Phenomenal, Powerful Inspirational Women—What's Their Claim to Fame?

Phenomenal, Powerful Inspirational Women— What's Their Claim to Fame?

I Added a Little Extra Spice to Feast Your Eyes On.

Daydreamer

Copyright © 2019 by Daydreamer.

ISBN: Softcover   978-1-7960-2799-0
               eBook   978-1-7960-2798-3

Print information available on the last page.

Rev. date: 04/15/2019

To order additional copies of this book, contact:
Xlibris
1-888-795-4274
www.Xlibris.com
Orders@Xlibris.com
792052

CONTENTS

Behold the Phenomenal Power of Women
and How They Should Be Loved
—And a Little Extra

Preface

Let's enter the realm of some amazing ladies and see what we can unfold.

The unique power only a woman possesses.

The value of a woman.

The intelligence of a woman has no boundaries.

The unique character of a lady.

The value of selecting a mate.

Trials and errors of a woman's life.

The beauty of a woman isn't just physical.

Gorgeous, flawed, spicy—all the right ingredients.

Beautiful, sultry, independent women with a heart of gold.

Rhymes of love and pain of life.

Before we begin to read, this book is part 1 of a two-part series.

This is the concluding chapter in the series.

To understand some of the events that were depicted in this version and the lives of some of the characters, I suggest you read the first book, *The Tranquility of Life Ablaze*, first to get a full understanding.

Prologue

Who holds the level of power, men or women?

Are famous people's stories more important than those who have no claim to fame?

Let's take a ride, a ride through the lives of women who had their own claim to fame, who were ignored because the media ignored their success in life because they lack a famous name.

The power of women uncompromising.

Women born in sin but doesn't use it as a excuse for not reaching their objectives in live.

Chapter One

Women of Power

Men are strong and brave, and they drive fast race cars at the speed of light. Their bravery is unprecedented because they fight in foreign unknown wars to protect our freedom.

Nothing is tougher or mightier than a man on a mission.

Men have conquered the moon and scaled Mt. Everest, but he's nothing without a woman because he needs her to take the splinter out of his hand as he lies down in a manger with a pacifier between his lips, crying like a baby.

A man could never carry a baby for nine months. Just the thought of it would send him into shock, rendering him helpless as a baby.

A woman is exquisite in her design, ever so beautiful and graceful, and comes in all sizes and shapes. And let's not deny her power to love and forgive without hesitation men who rains evil down on them.

The beauty of a woman does not rely on her features or the shape of her body. It's realized in the charm of her mind and her character. It doesn't matter what culture she came from. We love them all the same.

A woman's power is undeniable if used properly.

Many women fail to understand the power they have in their midst.

Let's discover some examples how some women used their power to achieve their objectives.

We heard about the fearless and bravery of the heroic Samson; no man or beast could bring him to his knees.

Then came the beautiful Delilah, who stole his heart and made him fall in love with her. But she pretended to love him only to find out the source of his strength.

She was sent by the Philistine to be cunning and deceitful for Samson to relinquish the source of his power.

Three times she failed to extract the information from him. But on the fourth attempt, she was successful because she summoned Samson's trust genes. She questioned him whether he loved or trusted her, then he fell sway to her, seducing his mind and body.

Delilah discovered the strength was in his hair by the drunk in love murmurings of Samson.

She had servant girls cut his hair while he was sleeping, thus, sapping him of his strength.

The power of a woman can make you feel invincible, or it can have you tied to columns in disgrace.

Samson fell sway to the love of a woman who was only out for herself.

This eventually brought about the death of Samson as he gained his strength back and brought the pillars down on himself and the Philistines.

Delilah achieved her objective, how much more Samson could have been if he didn't allow his desires to control his mind.

The power of a woman has no limits; how greater it would be if it was used to inspire greatness.

Let's think about the power of Eve.

Adam had the power of the world in his hand, but he undeniably disobeyed God for the love of Eve and lost it all.

He lost his stay in the Garden of Eden and was cast out to live and die like a common man because he chose to love Eve.

It's no doubt God would've given Adam another woman since Eve was deceived by the serpent, but Adam foolishly disobeyed God for the undying love of Eve. A true Romeo and Juliet.

The power of a woman is undeniably impressive.

Let's learn about the great feats of some modern day women in our time.

We have heard of women of fame like Oprah and Amy Winehouse; and let's not forget the bark of Wendy Williams; and I love me some Janet Jackson and Chante Moore.

What about the athletic genius of Marion Jones, Sanya Richards, Allyson Felix, and the great feats of Wilma Rudolph, Evelyn Ashford, and Jackie Joyner Kersee. Let's not forget the champions and record breakers Serena Williams and Laila Ali, and Chris Evert Lloyd, Dorothy Hamill, and Dominique Dawes.

How about those up-and-coming newcomers such as Naomi Osaka, Simone Biles, Gabby Douglas, Simone Manuel, and Lea Neal.

Oh yes, and the beauty of Salli Richardson, Denise Nicholson, Jayne Kennedy, Barbara Eden, and Linda Evans who put chills up many men's spines.

We've seen the beauty of Sophia Loren and Raquel Welch and Elizabeth Taylor in pictures as a child.

Then as we grow up into womanhood, we saw a new generation of women in films like Michelle

Pfeiffer, Meg Ryan, Demi Moore, Scarlett Johansson, Jennifer Lawrence, and how about those Oscar winners like Halle Berry, Meryl Streep, and Regina King.

Sanaa Lathan and let's not forget the beauty of Dorothy Dandridge and the artistic greatness of Viola Davis, Glenn Close, Cicely Tyson, Gladys Knight, and the genius of Ellen DeGeneres and Maya Angelou and Sigourney Weaver is second to none.

We heard of the great deeds of Rosa Parks, Shirley Chisholm, and Harriet Tubman; but the black women of NASA fame were unprecedented because they were working in a predominantly white male work environment.

We've covered women names we know oh so well. Now, let's uncover some everyday sheroes who are not seeking fame and glory in this world. All they're looking to do is to survive in this ungodly world and be loved and show love.

Whose claim to fame is living every day as it comes, while allowing unforeseen occurrences to run its course.

Then picking up the pieces where they may fall to restore life again, where all hope had vanished.

A lady, who claims success, was utilizing her willpower to enhance her life and that of others she loved and came into contact with.

Let's begin by learning about an unknown shero!

Chapter Two

Darlene

Darlene, the lady who risked her life to save the life of her kids and baby sister.

From a fate that was set in stone already pronounced hopeless.

This sheroic mom didn't see the writing on the wall.

Darlene not only heard the fat lady sing. The fat lady was sitting on her chest, but Darlene threw the two-ton lady off and sprung into action and fought against the odds and flames of death to save her family from the coroner morbid denunciation.

Darlene left the coroner bewildered and tongue-tied because she stole five corpses from his grip.

Her only focus was saving her kids and her beloved baby sister who she helped raise.

She wasn't trembling with fear because she knew her task at hand was only to save her family by any means necessary, from the flames of death by the infamous bump in the night.

Darlene never thought about what to do—she just jumped into action.

All thinking would have slowed her down when time was of the essence.

Her split-second reaction is what makes sheroes.

Not once did she think about her own safety or scalding herself in the flames.

Darlene once did not stop to think, but only to save the lives of her kids and baby sister.

Darlene wore many hats, a bonafide chameleon, and she did what it took to provide a good life for her kids and the men in her life.

An excellent cook, interior decorator, carpenter . . . you name it, she did it in the name of survival for her family.

A lady who had to do the job of both man and woman.

Darlene put up walls, put down carpet and ceramic floors, all in the name of giving her kids and herself a decent life.

She was also a great dancer and had a tongue that could shrink a grown man back to his mother's womb.

She had no fear of man or woman.

A lady whose claim to success was utilizing her willpower to enhance her life and that of others that she loved and come into contact with.

No criminal elements could be found in her; only the will to do right by her family and those who came in contact with her.

A lady whose sense of style was second to none.

A lady who cared for the sick and feeble all her life, including her mom and dad.

Giving up her life to take on their life and illness.

After her father passed on and her mother had to be put in a nursing home for specialized care, she moved back to her own home and started her life over.

The death of her father literally brought her to her knees. Most likely his death brought back the sad memories of her oldest sister who passed on from cancer and the baby girl who couldn't withstand the ferocious flames and blinding smoke from the bump in the night.

Darlene is the prime example of why you can never say "you can't do it."

Darlene and her oldest sister Betty we're like twins. Some people couldn't tell them apart. Betty was a beloved lady who was gone way to soon from that dreadful disease, cancer.

We will discuss her zeal to live right after Laya.

The pain and suffering from death never ends; it gets easier as time passes but it never ends.

Losing someone is an unnatural feeling; a feeling that no man or woman can never prepare for unless you were born insensitive.

Darlene started her life back over.

At an age when she should've been traveling and enjoying life, she had to adopt her great-grandson because the mother lost her rights and the father was serving time.

Darlene's escapades continued because not only was she taking care of her great-grandson because his mother lost her rights but because she allowed her firstborn son to be abused by the mother's boyfriend in the name of trifling love.

Cedric Jr. was repeatedly hit with a plastic bat around his body and head.

Upon his dad finding out, he immediately circled the apartment complex with his brothers and friends searching for the culprit.

A beat down was about to commence.

It was to no avail he was only brave when he was hitting a little boy.

When it came to him standing up against a man to show how brave he was, he took the coward's way and the safe way out.

His dad Cedric Sr. had to go away to jail for infraction of the law not related to this incident.

That's why Darlene became the main caretaker of Cedric Jr. because his parents were stripped of their rights. Todd was the guy who abused Cedric Jr.

He finally had his day in court when Darlene recognized who he was. She walked up to Todd and said, "Now beat and kick me like you did Cedric Jr.

"Look at me cross-eyed if you want, so I can show what I'm about."

Todd looked in disbelief; he hadn't thought about the possibility of getting beat down by a grandmother.

The revenge of Great-granny was put on hold.

The sheriff stepped in and stopped my mom from beating him and his parents down.

That's one thing you don't do is mess with her family.

To abuse a defenseless child is animalistic and a person who does that lacks a moral compass.

My mom took on extra responsibility when she should've been seeing the world and enjoying her life.

No, Darlene was tied down to taking care of Cedric Jr. and taking care of her now sick husband.

Darlene waited on her husband hand and foot. She wasn't about to leave his fate to the nursing home because in her mind that would be sure doom.

Think about how it had to weigh on Darlene to see her husband helpless and crying and talking as a baby and still give him his dignity as a man.

By no means an easy task, but she did just so she undoubtedly went past the call of honor.

A quest most women would've said, "I love, but I cannot do anymore," and no one would've blamed them under the circumstances.

Mother was no stranger to taking care of individuals.

When I was a kid, my mom always made sure we had the cleanest and finest clothes money can buy.

You notice I didn't say name brand.

We wanted to wear different outfits during the week, not just one or two outfits.

Mother always had the girls looking prissy and smelling all fresh.

With their hair all laid out and stylish.

It took Mother a little more effort when it came to me because I had developed a skin rash.

I believe it was caused by Agent Orange when my dad was in Vietnam.

Agent Orange is an herbicide and defoliant chemical, widely known for its use by the US military as part of its herbicidal warfare program, Operation Ranch Hand, during the Vietnam War from 1961 to 1971.

What other ways Agent Orange affected me, I probably would never know for sure.

For whatever reason, legal actions were never pursued and that information was never presented to me.

As a grown man, I never approached my dad because I didn't want to make him feel more guilty than he already felt.

My mother used to scratch all scabs out of my head; scabs would be flying everywhere, and they would be all over her and me.

There is the chiropractor that was treating Mom for her separated shoulder, which she incurred in the burning teepee that night when we all simultaneously cried out loud out of fear than the pain from burning.

The chiropractor that cared for Mom made a sab for my head.

It used to help some to bring the color back to my forehead but it never totally healed me.

My forehead used to be covered with white crusty scales that if you scratch would get worse. It would become reddish and sore.

Now picture a loving mother having to look at her extremely handsome son this way.

Just a little conceited . . . not really, because it took me a long time to feel good about myself.

Try to think about a young boy's head flaring up in school with these scaly, white patches.

Kids will be kids. I took it on the chin a lot of days.

It made me go inward somewhat shy because at times I had no idea how I appeared to others.

My dad and mom feverishly did everything they could to keep my rashes under control.

Time was the only cure.

I still have minor flare-ups but not as bad.

Mother continued her quest to find an answer to my condition alone once she and Dad divorced.

A lady of class and fortitude; a lady to be reckoned with; who can stick their hand in fire and come out unscathed and who made mockery of death.

Who on one hand can guide a youth through the trials of life and on the other hand fight hospice day and night to keep the coroner away—the one and only the Glamorous Diva Darlene.

This lady one day can be laying floor tiles or painting cabinets or putting up wallpapers.

The next hour you can see Darlene dressed to kill, so to speak.

The Mother of all Diva's give Darlene her due; bow when you see her because she is truly a natural queen, not one made up in fairy tales.

A lady who takes second to no one and more beautiful than precious pearls and more graceful than a dove.

A lady who gave respect and demanded it in return.

Behold her beauty as she walks by. Look at the jealous women poking their men's

eyes out.

She was tested and tried but no one or no enemy could overthrow her throne.

Long live, Queen Darlene.

Chapter Three

Kala

Kala is the spitting image of her mom Darlene. They are both beautiful women—not a self-proclamation but the official word in the streets.

Some say they must be twins—a claim to fame that would make no woman ashamed.

Their lives revolve around each other; there's nothing they wouldn't do to make the other comfortable mentally or physically.

They have a bond stronger than guerilla glue. No tsunami or words of slander, whether truthful or not, can break their bond.

Kala have had more than her share of hardships.

From deadbeat baby daddies to husbands lacking the faithful and true genes.

From her boys breaking her down with their unsavory way of financing their lifestyles.

At one point in her life, she became so stressed she was admitted to the hospital. There they discovered she was having baby strokes on the regular.

What was she to do when in life you inherit stress?

She would go on living her life and bonding with her boys to tie their hearts to what is righteous.

One thing I can say is they are unified as a unit.

No one will go hungry or do without food; no kid of theirs will wear nothing less than the best.

Being an underprivileged kid is nothing their kids will ever experience.

Doing one of my downtimes, Kala allowed me to lay my head at her home.

I was treated with royalty.

Not one time did she ever complain about loaning me money or say I was cut off, she couldn't be there for me no longer.

Do you know what hearing those words do to a person?

That in his or her life they prided themselves on being at others' beck and call without hesitation.

It destroys your insides, it make you feel worthless and unloved.

It's important to feel like someone has your back, no matter if you need it or not.

Kala has never let life's atrocities stop her in her tracks. She keeps moving even though at a tender young age her innocence was violated.

Kala was knocked off her bike and raped. How your life can change in a split second.

The pain she had to feel psychologically—what will people think, will they blame her, or will she be embraced and told, "Baby, I got you. We got you as a family." Isn't that the way it was supposed to be?

She was faced with the choice of aborting her baby, but she couldn't find it in her heart to kill a baby that was growing inside her.

Imagine the agony of facing such a dilemma.

Imagine her baby boy coming of age, and she has to tell him how he originated on earth.

Imagine the tears, imagine the feeling of low self-worth. Now feel the love that was shown this young man; it was nothing his heart desired that he was denied.

As he was spoiled, he was used to getting his way in life. Still, he had to deal with the fact he was fatherless.

How did he answer to other kids when they asked about his dad?

Did it cause anger or sadness? Did it make him feel lost, different, or was it all of the above?

It's no way we can duplicate his pain.

Or the pain of his mother.

Having empathy for someone doesn't mean they have the right to go in life unchecked.

The act of love involves guidance; and training a boy to be a responsible man in a confused world . . . imagine having that task.

We tend to overcompensate when we feel someone is grieving inside when we don't know how to answer the call of pain.

Often we try to smother the pain with material things, which acts only as a pacifier. It doesn't cure the call of pain.

As my uncle once told me, it's all about love and love of family.

Kala had a long journey ahead of her. How is it that someone has the audacity to plan your future without your permission?

One time, before Kala was ran down by a car coming from swimming pool this time, she *only* came away with a sprained ankle.

His purpose was to abduct her, but it was to no avail because Kala smartly jumped out of the way, causing her to land on a ditch causing her to sprain her ankle and causing the would-be abductor to flee the scene.

I said *only* because that was good compared to the first time when she got raped.

Kala doesn't reflect on the past but concentrates on her future and that of her boys: Brad the youngest, James the middle child, and Cedric the eldest.

She's in a constant fight to show her boys the right road to choose.

She not once gave up on what most people would consider a lost cause.

As long as there's breath then there is hope, she often says.

It's no doubting the sincerity of her love for her family at large.

A woman who only wanted to be loved and treated like a queen, which she was born to be.

She was royal in the way she wore her hair.

She was royal in the way she modeled her dress.

She was royal in the way she smiled.

She was royal in the way she loved.

She was royal in all ways. No one could deny she was a true queen.

Chapter Four

Laya

A beautiful lady who had endured things no child or woman should ever have to go through even in times of war.

She had been abused without mercy, sexually and physically.

First she was sexually abused by a man who came into our lives to pick up the broken pieces left by the divorce of our parents.

Unfortunately, he used his goodwill as a mask to wreak havoc in our lives.

Laya also had to endure the brutal beatings of her husband who used love as an excuse for his blows of pain to make up for his lack of manhood.

Her only guilt was being, and that's something she had no say in.

The love she has for her kids and for herself extinguish the pain she felt physically and mentally.

Not to say she doesn't have remnants of the past that attack her thoughts from time to time.

Like the loss of two sisters: one was her fraternal twin with whom she swam in her mother's womb, while the other died tragically by fire that razed by a bump in the night.

Pain that will never relinquish its hold in our hearts.

Laya's love of life and need to give back did not allow the disappointments in life to give her a mental meltdown. She strived to help other abuse victims find their peace in life.

A lady who never felt she had the support or love of her immediate family had been successful beyond leaps and bounds.

No, she's not rich or famous by society's standards, but she is by her character.

A lot of abused women resort to drugs and prostitution. They become promiscuous to pass the time of day to ease the pain in their heart and mind only momentarily, to repeat the cycle time and time again because they're not dealing with the pain but only feeding it.

Laya have had to sleep in cars and shelters, but not once did she succumb to being a sewer dweller.

Laya had been able to adlib where needed. She's been able to bypass the negatives of the past and picked out the positive experiences and lessons from the adults in her youth who were and still are dear to her.

Laya as a child dreamt to be a doctor, but she would settle for being an EMT but it didn't come to fruition. She wasn't crushed, maybe just a little disappointed. But she knew other opportunities would present themselves, so she never felt sorry for herself or gave herself outlandish pity parties.

I remember a time when we both went to this medical training center to ask questions about eligibility to get into this institution.

When we began talking, the medical instructor was amazed with our knowledge and how articulate we were, being so young.

At that time, we had the world in our hands; nothing was going to stop us.

Unfortunately, we had to take a breath and start living life as we watched helplessly as it changed our course.

Was Laya mentally stressed? Yes. Was her mind nonstop like the Georgia highway? No doubt.

How did she cope with all the traffic in her mind?

She put stoplights in her mind to free up the traffic in her mind.

To turn the flow of traffic in a positive direction, so she could be of benefit to others.

She decided to help the unfortunate, the distraught, the distressed, and those who thought their life was decomposed.

Laya was helping herself by helping others. She started an organization for abused women, giving hope where there were no choices.

In life, we are forced to walk on broken glass. From the pain, we find courage to walk on from courage, we come into our strength which empowers our will to not succumb to life's pain receptors.

If we succumb to the mental and physical pain in our life, then our courage cannot nourish our will effectively to go forward properly.

Thank you, Laya, for bypassing your pain to grace us with your wisdom you learned through your agonies in life.

No one glorifies pain. We use it to enhance our stamina to speed walk through the troublesome times in life.

Laya is a proud mother of three girls and one son, who all benefited from her diligence to never succumb to life's walk of pain.

Laya's dream is to become an abuse counselor to empower women to never give but step up and fight back and be heard and be counted among the living. She had given life back to the forgotten.

Laya has three beautiful daughters.

Who endured the drama of their brother and mother, being physically abused with no power to equal the equation.

Let me introduce them to you one at a time.

Chapter Five

Kahlea

Their beauty is their weakness because its uncontrollable.

The youngest lady, Kahlea, has two beautiful kids, a boy and a girl.

Her adversity in life is not of her doing.

She gave into her love by saying I do to the man she had willed her life to.

It's now evident that his commitment was spoken but not engraved in life.

Shortly after their divorce, he returned to his roots of playing hide and seek with the cops with a blindfold on.

He's now doing over ten years for failure to putting his wife's needs before his.

Now she has to struggle on her own to raise her two kids.

A job she doesn't take for granted nor does she think it's a hindrance to her life going forward.

A beautiful body is nothing without character and an attached mind.

This young lady has it all and a strong will—a force to be reckoned with.

She knew life never promised her a rose garden with no thorns.

That's because she is a rose, and she learned to live among the thorns and keep her beauty of mind.

Her story is ongoing. She passed up a chance to be a track star to put all her efforts into getting a college degree, thinking it would be more advantageous than putting her hopes in making a living running, not knowing how far should would go. No doubt she had mad skills on the track field, but your heart have to be in it to win it all.

The youngest of her two sisters whose story as I said is yet to unfold.

The world judges success by one's accomplishment in life, by one's win or lose record.

I judge accomplishments by how I live my life and what effect I have on others' achievements.

Kahlea thought that pattern is much the same. She's not worried about seeking her own glory but that of her kids, enhancing their lives and living through their achievements.

A star she is, without the fame and glitter.

If you ever get a chance to meet her, ask her for her autograph because it's no doubt you would swear she's a beautiful movie star.

It's all about having class and how you carry yourself. You don't need a star on the Walk of Fame to realize you're a star on the move.

Now let's meet her middle sister.

Chapter Six

Ereca

Ereca who excelled in whatever she did, but her gift was the love in her to give back.

She always had a job and made sure her daughter was safe and well taken care of.

Her love was contagious and her heart goal was to show compassion where it had been depleted.

The man in her life wasn't her equal because he squandered her love by living a life that was amoral and selfish, not understanding he had opened the door to paradise.

Ereca needed to feed humanity with her love. She allowed a man with no future goals to feed off her love without returning it to sender.

Ereca is a remarkable mother who didn't allow the remnants of her abusive father to rule her life.

Her willingness to try to heal the man she loved even though he was standing out of bounds, out of the play of love proved that her pain of abuse was introverted as she would've never wasted her time saying hi. Her love was blinded by the need to heal.

Maybe it was her need to find closure from her father.

Ereca's beauty of heart continues to strive even though the stress in life's forecast is unending rain.

Ereca's umbrellas of love allow her to go on unimpeded through the acid raindrops.

My nieces have been battling the steps of life, but they cease to let life limit their growth. I can't say it enough—they are simply beautiful women.

Chapter Seven

Valencia

My nephew is striving to overcome his history of abuse and become a man who inspires greatness.

Shay, my nephew, found out he needed an organ transplant himself.

Upon hearing this, his sister Valencia took to the road to share her kidney.

Of Shay's plight, Valencia had no doubts; she knew what she had to do—preserve her brother Shay's life.

Ereca, the second-oldest, followed her in case Valencia wasn't a match, because she would be next in line to take Valencia's place.

Kahlea was on standby in case Valencia and Ereca were not a match.

The doctor was amazed at such selfless love as we all should possess.

Valencia wasn't crying or sad about going under the knife. She was ecstatic because she could extend her brother Shay's life.

She was ready on day 1, not knowing if she would be a match—what selfless love! Could you do such?

This was such a beautiful and heart-warming story. Valencia never once questioned her love.

Laya and her kids were conquering life one day at a time, keeping focused and not looking back or making excuses for lost time.

Laya has overcome a lot of obstacles and has become a strong woman who didn't allow being victimized by society's definition of who she was destined to be.

She has yet to recognize the power of her beauty; it wasn't significant in her achievements in life.

Valencia's beauty brought people to her, then they were astonished by her mind.

This allowed people to see the depth of her heart wherein love swam, unabated by hate.

A lady whose future has already taken shape and is very promising.

A star she has become because she illuminates all that's around her.

Beauty can be a hindrance if it's too heavy for you to carry. The weight of beauty is in believing your strength is not in your beauty but in your mind.

It is an accomplishment that all these women share in common. Valencia is a beautiful lady who gave birth to a handsome young man.

A lady whose beauty transcends and encompasses any other achievements she must have locked away in her portfolio.

A lady who is an actress and a model.

One of her greatest achievements and acts of love was when she forsook the safety of her life goals that was engraved in stone, to make sure her brother could continue his quexceptionalt.

Most people shrill out of fear by the thought of having a flu shot, but to be happy and gleeful about donating a kidney for transplant to make sure someone else can see the sunrise is unheard of.

She had no guarantees of success, but that didn't matter.

This lady was on the road along with her middle sister to make sure her brother would have a chance to continue breathing and doing all the things in life he found joy in.

Her self-sacrifice was felt by the surgeon who did the procedure, a point worth repeating.

He said he hadn't seen anyone with so much joy in going under the knife at a risk to their on life.

She wasn't an exact match for her brother but her selflessness had a ricocheting effect that saved five lives.

Indeed a marvelous gesture of love.

I listened to this young lady talk live one day on Facebook.

All I can say is she is awesome, and her message exuded love and was inspirational to all who listened.

Whether she becomes an actress or a model or an inspirational speaker on her syndicated talk show, her star is already engraved in life.

The beauty of life in life is not letting boundaries stagnate you.

Oh yeah, how did I forget that my niece Valencia is an inspiring star?

She has a movie she is working on.

Watch out, now a new star is rising.

Let it be noted that all three beauties were prepared to go under the knife to preserve their brother's life.

Laya and her radiant daughters continue their quest in life without making excuses and not looking back, as they continue their glory walk in the future.

Much love to four beautiful women.

I give my love and heart to my sister Laya, to my nieces Valencia and Ereca and Kahlea, and my nephew Shay.

May the work of your hands and heart allow you to prosper endlessly and stay healthy because you has been given a gift of love to continue life!

Chapter Eight

Betty

Betty and Mom were true patriots of the heart. Some thought they were twins.

I guess the fact that we were so used to seeing them together we didn't see the resemblance as some did.

Betty was married; she has three kids, a boy and two girls.

At one point in our life, we stayed right across the street from their house.

Mom and Aunt Betty always had their heads together.

They supported each other to the fullest.

Aunt Betty was the older of the two. If she

felt she needed to counsel Mom about something, she,didn't hesitate in doing so.

Aunt Betty was stern but loving; always had something encouraging to say.

A lady that had tremendous strength; after the passing of her husband, she didn't give up on life.

She put her positive energy on her kids.

All her kids were honor students, over achievers, very smart, I'm proud to say.

The one time my aunt got to me is when we were out, and she said she wanted a ride back with her nephew even though she came with someone else.

Why did that touch me so much because my oldest aunt had terminal cancer, and she knew she only had a certain amount of time left to live.

For her to want to spend some of that time with me meant the world to me.

Aunt Betty made sure she came to see Mom several times before she passed.

Her youngest daughter, the sweetheart that she is, made sure her mom's wishes were granted before she passed.

Aunt Betty was part of the glue that held our family together.

When you lose a patriarch as she was it no way a family won't suffer.

Aunt Betty never stopped working even though she only had weeks left to live.

Aunt Betty didn't let cancer take over her mind; she continued living life as normal.

A lot of people give up and give in to the thought of having cancer.

Aunt Betty's strength was admirable. She showed no signs of giving into the effects of cancer.

Cancer brings on pain, fatigue, nausea, and emotional stress.

How amazing it was for Aunt Betty for not allowing cancer to ravish her mind like it did her body.

How amazing it was that she found the strength to continue to work in public as if saying to everyone, no matter what it is that befalls us, don't give up; the fight has just begun.

She meant she was going to make the Grim Reaper earn his keep.

Aunt Betty was very pretty. She had cold-black silky hair and a will that could bend steal.

A lady that couldn't be tried with dishonesty or greed.

She made sure her husband and kids and grandkids were well taken care of, mentally and physically, by her exemplary example on how she carried herself.

Aunt Betty was truly loved by all who had a loving spirit. How could you not love a pillar of strength that helped power the engine to our family tree.

Now let's discuss a lady that's the epitome of strength. The lady we all came from, and whose wisdom and courage we had no choice but to inherit.

The difference is how we chose to you use it.

Chapter Nine

Natalie

Natalie is her name; a lady that had the lock on glamour and class.

A lady that was devoted to her husband and kids.

A lady that had been ill ever since I learned to say grandma.

Not once did she renege on her role as a loving mother or wife.

A lady, who when she could no longer stand, would slide up in her easy chair and continue to cook for her husband and kids and grandkids.

We would have family fun time when my aunts and uncle would gather to celebrate the meaning of wedded bliss.

My uncles would basically provide the food and entertainment along with Aunt Sonja.

My aunties would be cooking alongside their mother.

What a fine example of love they have shown by the blending of different personalities.

An example of love that has been lost in time.

Who forgot to push the send button on Love to our generation?

Indeed, time does change because we allow our standards of yesterday become old and outdated.

But the fact is love is everlasting; it always renews itself automatically.

My grandmother always did so. She was not perfect. She had to use a walker because of the pain in her legs and thighs; but yet and still, she didn't feel sorry for herself by lying on a bed of remorse.

My grandmother didn't give up on life after losing her husband and oldest daughter to that dreadful cancer.

Indeed, she was in emotional pain.

The pain of not being able to say the proper goodbye because she was too sick to attend the funeral.

Not that she wasn't willing to risk her health.

Her overprotective sons and daughters pulled rank and wouldn't allow her to attend because they thought it would be to emotionally draining for her.

Was it the right choice?

Should Grandma have had the right to choose her destiny?

When one person controls everyone in the family central heartstrings, then you do what it takes to call a munity and do what it take to preserve family.

Grandma was grief-stricken, but she survived to carry on her legacy of love and compassion, guiding us to the promised land of Love of Family!

Not one of my uncles or aunties was convicted of a crime.

To raise ten kids and not one turn to a life of crime speaks volumes.

When you can't hardly raise one kid in the age of technology and social media, to have respect for themselves and adults.

What did my grandmother and grandfather do that was different than today?

They parented and showed love. They taught their kids life skills when there was no Xbox or Super Nintendo.

Today the kids got the worldwide web at their fingertips, but somehow they find life boring so they choose to be disrespectful and call on crime to cure their boredom.

Even though they jumped over racism and segregation and have all the wonders of technology and the convenience of the fire stick and cable and its hundreds of stations and counting.

My aunties and uncles used to put a clothes hanger at the back of a black and white TV screen to get reception from a TV with three channels.

Not saying kids today are not faced with the effects of racism, but do you really want to compare the times?

What made my grandmother special is her love for mankind, not just her family.

If she could do something to enrich your life, she would do so with maximum speed.

Granny was special because her advice was on point and still relevant today.

She was special because the taste of her food was intoxicating and addictive you could never get enough.

I have yet to taste someone's food that even came close.

Grandma was an exceptional cook compared to other grandmas.

She was indeed an exceptional cook.

It's no doubt in my mind if she had marketed some of her recipes, she would have her own food label.

Grandma put love in her cooking. She took the time to cook it right.

There was no microwave or TV dinners. I can just taste her homemade biscuits, pies, and cakes.

Grandmother kept her secret recipe in the family. Even though my mother and aunts learned to cook from her, they weren't on her level.

Grandma was also a great interior decorator.

Most likely from her Sonja learned her skills as a flower decorator.

Grandma taught by example; she just didn't spit out words.

There was nothing my grandmother's heart desired that she didn't get.

Grandmother was getting sicker, and it was hard on my aunts and uncles so they decided to put her in a nursing home.

It was hard because Granny took care of us all. How in their audacity could they have come to that conclusion?

They all had their own families; they were struggling with their on health issues.

In no way was it a unanimous decision but the fact that Grandma needed specialized care took precedent.

For the backbone of the family not to recognize her oldest son or daughter who loved her dearly also took a toll on them.

For your mom not to recognize or look at you as an intruder has to hurt deeply.

No amount of trying to convince her or showing her pictures of the present and the past can change the equation.

We have to do whatever we need to do to proceed and make sure Grandma is loved. One thing for sure, she may have forgotten us but we know who she is, and we have to continue to do our part no matter how it hurts to see her in that position.

There's no way in the world would she have given up on us.

She proved all throughout life she had been a pillar of support.

Even in the state she was in, she exuded greatness and the will to comfort and to show compassion to those whose souls are being torched.

My grandmother exhibited the qualities that set the bar for us to achieve.

Grandma was responsible—she had to be because she raised over seventy-five kids including her children, grandkids, and great grandkids.

She was honest and patient, supportive of our views but without hesitation would set us straight on a dime.

So what caused her memory lost?

Was it a chemical imbalance?

Was it an accumulation of emotional and physical pain over the years?

Was it when she got the call when her baby girl had suffered first-degree burns in a horrific car accident?

What toll that had to take on her mind; a mother's job is to soothe and heal, but she had no power to do either. How that had to wreck her mind.

What about the death of her oldest daughter? A pain I know she still feels something for and that memory loss cannot erase.

What about the love of her beloved husband, the love of her life, who she had been married to over fifty years? It was a loss that maybe set everything in motion because she wanted to let the pain in her mind sleep.

Add in the loss of her mother and siblings, then you know the toll was too great to bear.

A fascinating woman.

A very beloved woman.

I know I haven't given her the credence she deserves, but I just wanted you to get to feel her love as we all have.

Grandma's caregivers can attest to who she was as a person.

Chapter Ten

Aunt Sylvia

I can remember when I was graduating, and Aunt Sylvia and Mom had took me out far in the county to find me a suit.

We had gone to several stores when I finally found one I liked but it was too pricey.

My mom didn't have enough money. My aunt so as not to disappoint took care of the situation.

I was the best dressed at my high school graduation.

My aunt was a fantastic seamstress she could make anything.

I remember her making me a two-piece red-and-white checkered outfit,

for that era I was the stuff you couldn't tell me I wasn't looking good.

My aunt with the help of her sisters made gowns for several weddings.

Why she never went national is a mystery to me.

You now know the effect Grandma had on her kids. They felt there was nothing they could not achieve because not one was left behind without confidence.

Aunt Sylvia also had to raise three kids and haul down a job at the same time being a caregiver to her parents.

Grandma was basically bedridden when Granddad got cancer, but she did what she could.

Aunt Sylvia worked tirelessly to help her dad keep his dignity because he was a very proud man.

A man that built his house from the ground up and added an elevator when his wife was unable to walk out the house on her own strength.

My grandma was treated as a queen, and she had the life and home of a queen. She was denied nothing within my grandfather's power.

Every last one of the girls took a part in caring for their parents.

It took a great toll on their emotions going forward.

No one should question anyone's love or capabilities. Everyone cannot take the same emotional pressure.

Whether you are hands-on or helping financially, you are taking an active part.

The danger comes in when you start to judge someone's motives or heart condition.

It's no doubt in my mind my aunts and uncles did all they could for their parents.

No one can judge the heart motivation, the only thing we should be concerned if we are doing all we can.

Chapter Eleven

Aunt Bernice

I remember when me and Dad had a disagreement that didn't originate between me and him.

I got angry and moved in with my cousins.

It was my graduation year. It was supposed to be special—a fond memory to look back to.

My aunt and cousin did all they could to make it memorable.

Again, like in my eighth grade graduation, I was without a suit.

My cousin was graduating at the same time as I was.

He was more than happy to let me wear his brand-new suit.

He was a little taller than I was; he made good use of his height.

He was the star basketball player on his high school team.

One of the greatest one-on-one player I have ever seen.

The most fierce athlete I had ever seen play that includes the NBA.

I went on to graduate with the love of my aunt and cousin.

During the summer, my aunt's home was my hangout. I couldn't wait for the weekend to hang out with my cousins.

My aunt played her part in making sure her parents were well taken care of.

There was nothing they desired that they were deprived of.

All my aunts and uncles were pivotal in taking care of Grandpa and Granddad.

They were also pivotal in granting us a good childhood.

Chapter Twelve

Aunt Crystal

Me and my two older sisters went to Uncle Denzel and Aunt Crystal's house to stay when Mom had to go to the hospital for an operation.

I remember my uncle taking us shopping and buying us school clothes.

They would treat us out every weekend to Chinese food; we got to order anything we wanted.

I used to cut their grass. When I finish, Aunt Crystal would always fix me lunch; it was always delicious.

Aunt Crystal was a beautiful lady. She treated us like her own kids even though she was married into the family through my uncle.

Aunt Crystal had miscarriages; she lost a couple set of twins.

She sincerely loved kids.

Aunt Crystal had a very good job, but she wasn't able to keep it because she got really ill.

Even though she was sick, she never gave up on having kids.

Aunt Crystal eventually had a boy then later on two more girls.

Aunt Crystal having kids was a small miracle given the fact she had lost twins.

A testament to who she is and her willpower.

No kids can be shown more love.

My cousins took after their parents; they are very smart and loving. Society can only improve with my cousins at the helm.

My aunt and uncle truly loved kids. Look how they went out their way to take care of us.

My uncle always says it's about family, and that's true. If you don't have a family, what do you have?

Aunt Crystal is exceptional. She taught us a lot. The one main thing she taught us was what family was about based on how she cared for us like we were their own kids.

A lady of class and style, you cannot find any evil within her.

If you want to know how a man and woman should love each other, my uncle and aunt are prime examples why everyone should never miss the taste of love.

They had a fairy-tale love; the one you only see in movies.

Chapter Thirteen

Aunt Linda

Lost her husband to cancer. Did she shrink back in life and give up? No, she continued her wonderful life her husband afforded her.

I remember they used to take us on vacation with them and make sure we were well fed.

They used to organize picnics at the park.

Aunt Linda also took part in making sure her dad and mom got proper care.

Think how hard it was for her to balance being there for her mom and taking care of her dying husband.

They had one true love, and set an example how you should treat your mate.

Think how hard it was to sit down and tell her kids their dad only had a few days to live.

Think how hard it was to tell her son who was about to get married. How that had to destroy him.

The wedding proceeded, and it was the loveliest wedding I ever attended.

How hard it had to be for my cousin to be happy when he should have been crying. But he knew this day meant the world to his dad and mom because they got one last chance to love on each other.

My aunt made a way for her husband to be at the wedding.

To think one's life was ending and two new lives in love was on the horizon.

How much anguish they all must have been feeling.

The love my aunt and uncle showed by being in attendance when they could have

stayed at home, drowning in their misery.

No, they decided to give the best give that money can't buy. They gave of themselves.

They sacrificed their feelings so their son and new daughter can be happy.

My aunt showed how to be strong under duress. They all showed the true meaning of selflessness.

Chapter Fourteen

Carmelita

In life, we are often faced with many obstacles which often have us puzzled, saying, Why me?

What did I do wrong?

Why have I been cursed?

Unfortunate things happen to us not because we are bad, or God is having us pay back for some evil deed.

In life, we have trauma and drama and unforeseen occurrences giving birth at a moment's notice.

For no rhyme or reason, unforeseen occurrences happen.

At times, someone dear to us is the root of our distress; something that we can never prepare for.

The question is, how do you get through the thorny maze we find ourselves in as we walk through life without getting stuck?

We lick the wound because there's no way we want to get stuck. We just keep on moving and keep speaking to life our will to live.

Carmelita's life has been groomed in pain but she never said, "I give up!"

Not even after her father got cancer and got a voice box. She saw the agony that followed him day and night. She forged her pain but sought to give comfort to her dad to ease his time he had left on earth.

At another time in life, she had deal with one of the most trying times in her life but how she would not dignify her pain by giving up.

Her mother who was her life was in the hospital the same time she was with a mysterious disease that caused her skin to peel.

Carmelita was unable to see her mother because of the surgery she had. There is not a limit to the pain one person can have in their lifetime.

Let me tell you about a young lady named Carmelita. She said if her life wasn't traumatic, she wouldn't feel right.

Carmelita is overweight and has an eating disorder because she was violated at a young age by a family member.

She used food to comfort her stress and to try block out the pain.

Carmelita has not once given up on life or blamed God or anyone for her troubles in life, even though she has had about three lifesaving operations.

One time, she had to stay in a creepy nursing home for some months to recover from surgery.

She had to walk with a walker but she didn't consider herself handicapped because she still can get around and do what needed to be done without having a pity party.

Carmelita from time to time have painful boils that come on her body from Type 2 diabetes, which cause great pain. The healing process is not immediate because diabetes makes pain linger on. The healing process is slow because of neuropathy which makes it hard for blood to circulate for the needed skin repair.

In order for the boils on her stomach to heal, Carmelita had to be operated on, and they couldn't close her up; they needed to let her heal on her own.

Imagine having surgery and not being able to get staples or stitches.

Carmelita always found a new way to cope.

Her main way of coping was having faith in God.

Carmelita also have epileptic seizures, which cause her eyes to wail around in her head and causes her to black out. Not once had she given up on herself or her husband who is now critically ill with cancer.

So her baby sister had to be the caregiver; she also had to go see her mom and big sister at the brink of death.

A remarkable young lady and a remarkable feat that took its toll on her, still making sure her mom and sister were properly cared for; how heart wrenching.

Carmelita never got to see her mother before she passed away . . . how sad.

Carmelita's mother was her lifeline when she needed a hero. She would always come to her rescue but now she's gone. What is Carmelita to do?

In life you either buckle under pressure when the weight of the world is on your shoulders or you realize that life doesn't stop because of pain or death!

The pressure from the weight of the world can only weigh you down, if and when you it allow it to control your life and dictate your every emotion and action.

Carmelita lifted her head erect and took one step one day at a time to build her strength and faith up, so she could have the stamina to conquer any added weight on her shoulders.

It's called not giving in to the weakness in your mind, not giving up because that would be the easiest thing to do.

If you fall on one knee and feel all hope is gone.

Take a deep breath and don't give recognition to the fear that has weakened you at the knees.

I say rise up above it because it's only a momentary montage of illusory mirage to test the strength of your heart and mind.

Through tribulations, we gain strength to rise up and to fight again.

The sum of Carmelita's life and all the lovely precious ladies talked about so far is that they are fighters.

Carmelita is a bare-knuckle street fighter who has been sucker punched and knocked down to her knees, but she always found the strength to get up and fight fiercely without letup.

Carmelita is still fighting her illness to this day.

Carmelita had great hope as a young teenager.

She was an honor student in school.

Carmelite went to college to study medicine, but her health didn't let her stay.

Not once did she feel sorry for herself; had she done so, her life would've been over.

Carmelita has always been an inspiration to me—a lovely lady with the strength of mind like the power of mighty Hercules.

I love her dearly. Only if I could absorb her pain.

With the saying of Patrick Henry, her motto is "I haven't begun to fight."

This is true in life: what doesn't kill us helps us grow stronger, to focus on the next day, to lay waste to your problems at hand.

When we focus on our pain, we lose touch with reality then go into an abyss, unable to move forward.

When we recognize our pain but deny its power over us, we give oxygen to our lungs and renew our cells for future fights.

Strive on, my Queen. It's nothing your willpower can't sidestep and move past to finish your journey in life.

Chapter Fifteen

Rebecca

A beautiful lady who can be rude and loving in a split second of each other.

A lady who has no shame in speaking her mind, even when there's a loaded gun pointed to her head.

A lady so full of herself, Rebecca and her abilities can power up a nuclear plant with one breath.

Rebecca has two lovely kids. It's nothing she wouldn't do within her financial prowess to make her kid's life enriched.

Rebecca now finds herself divorced. She was married to the love of her life, from her childhood her dreamboat.

When you marry for love, your husband shouldn't become your adversary.

Her husband created adversity in her and her kid's life.

He had a very lovely wife who loved him and cared for him, even through his troubles with drugs and the law.

This lady walked in her stilettos to retrieve her husband from the drug houses to show him how much she loved him and need him in her life.

Rebecca had her choice of men; she didn't have to stay in a drowning situation.

But she did because she was dedicated to her man, and she wanted him hooked on her love and not on drugs.

It was said his problems arose from the childhood abuse he suffered in the hands of his uncle.

A problem he rode in life unchecked, taking him in the opposite direction of the land of virtue and honesty.

Rebecca knew in her wisdom she couldn't change a man who wasn't willing to change himself.

Rebecca had been through eye surgery to repair her retina. But it was not to be her eyesight that would allow her to see the beauty others could not see.

A lady who had to battle to keep her family together, with no help from her husband.

He was too busy on cocaine and getting drunk on alcohol, thinking he's the king of the world.

He often came walking down the street from his high, naked while eating a turkey leg, telling stories how he was abducted and left naked to suck on a turkey leg with nothing but Michelob-flavored saliva to wash it down.

To keep his high going, he would often find himself shoplifting or hijacking a car only to be caught and lying and saying he wasn't trying to steal the car, that he was trying to buy the car with a chicken wing and a supersized Slurpee that he had stolen.

That ordeal caused him to go away from his family and figure out why he had chicken wing and not an eight-piece to take to his family and hopefully wake him up to the wrinkles he was giving his lovely wife.

Rebecca couldn't trust him with the kids because she came home from work one day and found her baby boy outside on the porch, crying as he was left home alone.

Yes, it was the same day he was walking down the street naked with a turkey leg . . . Enough is enough, right!

Rebecca is an excellent cook and mother and wife. She had no known weakness or fault.

Well, let me rethink that she has a temper. She was never wrong. She won't let you get a word in edgewise when she's trying to prove a point. She would drown you out with her high-pitch voice even though she was often wrong but she would never admit to it.

A very sassy lady; a spitfire, to say the least.

Seriously! Rebecca is an amazing woman; a lady who should be classified armed and dangerous with a loud mouth.

She is one of a kind special lady.

Not really, but it sounds good to say.

She really is a very smart and resourceful lady. You couldn't go wrong with her on your team.

I don't think.

Rebecca is partially blind but carries on with her life like she has 20/20 vision.

Rebecca goes to work and do her job better than her workmates who have 20/20 vision and a magnifying glass.

She handles over a million-dollar budget without breaking a sweat.

No operation can change her eyesight, but that won't stop her from living a fun-filled life.

Not once has she given up on life even though she doesn't always get support within her circle.

When I first met Rebecca, I was amazed and inspired by how she dealt with her blindness. She didn't allow it to handicap her one bit.

Explain to me, how does a blind lady in stilettos lead you through a maze of paperwork of recorded deeds, and works on the computer day in and day out, yet is considered to be legally blind.

I guess Rebecca's boss can answer that being the fact she frequently directs his steps making him look good and in charge and in the know.

She runs the office; she worked in with precision.

Her coworkers are jealous because not only was she efficient in her job.

Rebecca was also stylish which called tension. They couldn't figure out why they can't compete with her on any level, even though they had 20/20 vision and she hadn't.

One thing was true: Rebecca didn't allow her handicap to direct her step.

A strong woman, no doubt. When I first met her, she was reading a book like it was attached to her eyelids. I was amazed because she acted like it was the norm. There was no shame in her game.

Rebecca never ever had consistent help from her kids' father. It didn't matter she was going to make sure her kids lived an enriched life and be well rounded.

Rebecca is a tried and true warrior. Nothing will stop this sassy queen's progress—not even an oversized turkey leg her thrown at her head.

Rebecca is now in the process of starting her catering business. No doubt, anything she puts her mind around will become a success; plus she's an excellent cook.

Maybe it's because she cannot see the ingredients. It's okay, you can laugh. She has a sense of humor. Her eyesight is not her weakness, rather it's her source of strength.

She doesn't believe in pity parties or in grieving past the setting of the sun.

She cannot be sidetracked or out talked.

Her survival tactic cannot be denied.

It is the reason why she still reigns over her kingdom and sits on her throne.

Chapter Sixteen

Vera

Is a prime example of someone who doesn't allow life's circumstances to give you an excuse for not achieving your best out of life.

She was brutally physically abused by her former husband.

She didn't wallow in self-pity or have pity parties for attention.

Vera took control of her life and that of her children.

Vera is a very detailed lady. She likes to control the day ahead of her, not allowing for failures of any kind.

Vera started work at sixteen and kept the same job some fortysomething years later.

Vera didn't let her severe back pain to stop her from carrying out her duties as a mother or housewife.

Neither was it an excuse for her to miss work.

She proved through hard work and determination that you can achieve anything you put your mind on.

Vera set the example for her three boys. She showed the meaning of hard work by setting a proper example.

Vera didn't allow her boys to say "I can't" or to make up an excuse not to succeed in whatever endeavor that opens its door. No, she didn't play that game. If you didn't want to hear the wrath of Vera, you better act like you got some type of game.

Vera is my stepmother; she was my dad's third wife.

I credit her with being an ultimate wife for sticking by my dad when she had good enough reason not to.

Dad was drinking too much and partying at the club with females who didn't resemble his wife, who was at home, waiting to have dinner with him.

Vera didn't turn her back on Dad when his heart stopped in the emergency room.

She didn't walk away from him when he was sick with cancer, and when he could no longer care for himself.

Vera and I were bosom buddies at one time, but time and differences in opinions in life eroded our friendship to a certain extent.

Vera not only took care of my dad. She made sure her ailing parents didn't suffer or want for anything.

For three months in a row, she had to drive sixty miles back and forth to make sure Dad was receiving proper care.

Believe me, you didn't want to witness the wrath of Vera by neglecting one of her loved ones.

I credit Vera with my dad's longevity in life.

No quitting! No self-pity! No pity party! No harmful speech in the atmosphere or thinking was allowed.

Vera felt if you spoke negative, then you gave power to negative energy. For whatever reason, no matter what dad was experiencing, she always said he was good.

That was her coping mechanism. Everyone copes in different ways; whatever wakes you up every day and allow you to have a productive day untarnished by negative vibes, then I say do you.

Her motto was not to give in to the cries of hopelessness.

My dad was put in hospice he had three days to live.

Vera buck the system; she became his will to live.

She fought and fought for his life until three days turned into two years later and up to this time, he is still alive.

I appreciate you very much for giving my dad a quality life befitting a king.

I love you for being selfish with your love to protect my dad from those who you didn't know what feelings they had stored in their heart for Dad.

We love who we love, not for the way they look or what they have in their bank account or what they can bring to the table.

We love who we love because they accept us for who we are; because they don't discriminate against us; because we lack perfection.

Chapter Seventeen

Sonja

My aunt Sonja always was the life of the party. She always made sure we were entertained and had fun when we were at family functions.

Aunt Sonja always played games with us or had talent shows, so we could showcase our skills.

She wanted us to enjoy our childhood. She didn't want us to grow up too fast and miss out on our childhood.

Aunt Sonja knew how kids were deprived for one reason or another and had to act as adults.

She didn't want that for us; she wanted us to enjoy our innocence as long as we could because she knew at a moment's notice it could be stolen from us, even with our eyes wide open.

I remember her taking us to eat and to the movies. She also took me shopping for school clothes; memories of love you cherish forever.

It was said by the doctors that Aunt Sonja would never have kids a result of a car accident where she broke her pelvis from the bump in the night that sent us up in flames.

Well that was proven false. She went on to have two beautiful girls and a handsome young man.

Not only did she have a broken pelvis, she had first-degree burns on her beautiful face as well.

Sonja's beauty is unquestionable; the flames only highlighted her beauty even more.

A lady who has magical skills. As a floral designer, she was second to no none.

Sonja would go on to coordinate a weddings and make it look so lavish that you would swear it was a movie star's wedding and not on Walmart budget. She was just that awesome.

Aunt Sonja would make time to make sure her kids and nieces and nephews knew what it felt like to be a kid who felt loved.

A lady who has made her mark in life by caring for and loving others. What greater gift can you give but love.

A million dollars can buy an act of love that will evaporate in air just like money will.

A loving memory lasts through generations, to be told over and over again, while not allowing that loving memory to die.

That's what my Aunt Sonja brought to my life. She made memories to look back to, to understand the joy life offers you.

I thank you for your love and fun memories of a lost time. Where did time go?

Can Replay be pushed and the hurt and pain be erased. Is that such a hard question to ask?

Chapter Eighteen

Jamie

Jamie is a young lady that has men's heads doing 360-degree turn with her unquestionable beauty.

She was in the transportation business by profession, but she gave it up to help her husband pursue his dream to be a restaurant owner.

Jamie showed her devotion to her husband and marriage by relocating and giving up her thirty dollar-an-hour job plus bonuses for a cause that wasn't concrete. But that's the call of selflessness seeking to do the will of your mate and allowing your life to simmer at the back burner.

A lady who was thought to be a model or actress of some sort.

Ladies envied her every movement, even though at the same time they wanted to be her, even though they didn't know what she has been through in her life.

The things like being an excellent wife, mother, and being a great homemaker are the things they should've wanted to emulate instead of her walk and astonishing beauty.

Some things you can't imitate, you got to be born with.

Jamie also was a great cook, who cooked everything from scratch like the grandma, but the only difference she was looking like a Victoria secret model while doing so.

A lady who is well endowed in more ways than one, and money is not the focal point.

Once you look upon her, you get the point.

A no-nonsense type of woman who demands respect from the men and women who surround her.

Jamie's father never played a pivotal role in her life, but nevertheless when he died, she didn't hesitate to make sure he had the proper burial and all his belongings and business were properly taken care of. That's the type of woman she was; she couldn't be tied to resentment as she felt it stunt your growth—never been more true.

She forgave her father for signing a contract with deadbeat dads of the world.

Jamie also forgave her two brothers for sexually abusing her as a girl.

She said how can she heal within if she can't forgive outwardly and freely letting go of the unending and unforgettable pain.

She just did so by allowing the younger of the two villains to reside with her when he became homeless and jobless. A heart of gold or is she naïve?

Her train of thought: you cannot return evil for evil and expect to prosper.

Sometimes you have to let people play their cards before you show your hand to see if they're showing a hand of strength or weakness.

He thanked her by staying drunk and continuing down a dark road of self-destruction.

Most likely, guilt was controlling his train of thought but not enough to apologize and accept responsibility of a unconscionable action.

Instead, he turned the tables on Jamie and tried to make her look questionable.

The fact is, if you plant weeds you can't expect to grow beautiful roses.

He continued down a life of debauchery.

When he had been forgiven, all he had to do is say thank you for giving me my life back and releasing me of my heinous sins.

I know now my heart can stop skipping a beat every time I lay eyes on you because of my shame that I lay unconcealed.

Nope. Accepting responsibility would've been the smart and not so easy thing to do, but he made his choice to go a crooked mile barefooted, which he now he travels down the dark side of life, shunning any type of responsibility.

The older brother of the two grieved himself to the point of committing suicide.

It's sad, he couldn't voice out his sorrows; he had to say it with his life.

In her heart, she found forgiveness because the pain of not forgiving would be too strong.

Something I couldn't even think of contemplating for one minute.

I often told her she was bigger than I could ever be; she had the true spirit of forgiveness.

In a situation such as this, I would outlaw in my mind because it would seem poisonous to my genes, to my very existence as a man.

Jamie is a true gem of a lady. She has showed me how it's possible to forgive and show compassion at the same time.

There's no way under the sun would I allow the man who sexually abused my wife knowingly reside under my roof without teaching him the consequences of his actions. I wouldn't be seeking revenge; I'd be seeking redemption for failure to pay his fine in immorality.

A lady in her early forties, with eight kids and who doesn't look a day over thirty.

She is a testament to her zeal for life and not letting trauma traumatize or stall her walk on earth.

A lady who finds beauty in everyone even if it can't be seen.

A lady who can make a valid excuse to spit on her life but no, she fights with every fiber in her body to fight for her kids and protect them from the evil that lurks in life.

For this very reason, we remained friends.

Her beauty made me take a second look, but her heart made me say, "Thank you for being my friend."

Beauty is fleeting; it seldom stays around until the end of your lifetime.

Jamie has plans to redirect the evolution of time.

She proved to be honest and a true-blue friend, one you just have to tell the world about.

Her beauty was honest; nothing fake or plastic or she had to take a pill for.

Her beauty was the cause of many women's envy, but she never paid it no mind because she thought everyone was beautiful.

I tried to tell her that wasn't true, but she looked and me and said, "Get real. Beauty is not superficial. Don't train your eyes for a certain look because love is blind to how a person looks."

Chapter Nineteen

Rachel

Rachel had the perfect family: a boy and a girl and a handsome husband.

They were an up-and-coming power couple.

Rachel was a very pretty and intelligent lady.

She was assistant CEO of a large food company.

Her husband held down a factory job.

Rachel also got hired at other companies to troubleshoot when they were in a financial crisis.

The world was at their doorstep. Rachel was embarking on opening her own financial consultant firm.

She would have several offices in local cities adjacent to where she lived.

Rachel got sick and had to have a major heart surgery; that's when the true color of her husband came out.

Instead of him staying on his job that had medical insurance, he decided to quit and work for his wife's financial service, which Rachel she started with her mother, leaving a question mark as to how Rachel was going to continue to have care over time.

Rachel made it through the surgery with the love of family and friends and at the skill of the doctor's hands.

Rachel and her husband Bob were on the rise; they had just purchased this five-bedroom home in this inclusive suburbs.

They had also just purchased a brand-new SUV.

Bob wanted a sports car so he goes out to buy one, but to his surprise the car dealer had to call his wife for approval because she holds controlling interest in the business she started with no help from her husband. Apparently, now he wants to reap the benefits and take charge.

Rachel had recovered and was doing fine. She was getting ready back to work.

She started to have people call the house and hang up.

She asked Bob about the calls. He claimed he had no idea why the calls were coming.

So the caller started to get bold and started asking for Bob. When Rachel would ask the caller's name, the caller would hang up.

Of course you know it was a female. This kept happening over time.

Bob was having affairs with women that came for financial consultation while in the office.

A friend of the family was spilling all the news, but Bob would continue to deny it.

Bob got sloppy. He got caught at an exclusive steak restaurant with a young lady.

Chaos soon followed because he continued to lie.

Rachel put a GPS on his car, so she could trace everywhere he went.

Bob was unaware of the GPS. Rachel confronted him at his mistress's house, but he lied and said he was doing some work for her.

Rachel wasn't buying that one bit; they had it out.

She made Bob pack his things and leave.

After news was out that they was splitting, Rachel was receiving all types of information about Bob.

One of Rachel's friends was visiting one of her close friends, and she wanted to share a picture of her new boyfriend. Yes, it was Bob.

Rachel soon filed for divorce.

Bob became disruptive, antagonistic, and revengeful.

Bob called the cops on Rachel. He said she had threatened his life and the girlfriend he didn't have.

Bob went as far as to withdraw all the money they had out of the bank account, leaving her kids penniless and no way to pay for utilities or mortgage.

What a swell guy. How do you pull the rug from under your on flesh and blood.

Rachel's mother had her back. She helped her out until the courts made Bob put the money back.

Bob wasn't done yet. He went after the house and the business that Rachel and her mother had started from the ground up.

Bob never actually did any work for the financial firm. He was just allowed to look important and pop in and out like he was the CEO.

While Rachel still had her secular job, Bob was roaming the streets free.

How can one be so inept? He had it made—a beautiful wife and two smart lovely kids.

Nothing was stopping them, but his ego and the need to be loved by any woman but his wife.

They had a contentious divorce that went on for about six years.

Rachel was granted all rental property and financial consulting business because she had acquired all that before they got married.

Rachel sold the house, and she was only required to give Bob interest from the sale of the house.

Rachel was saddened about the whole ordeal because she did truly love Bob.

On the other hand, Bob looked like an opportunist; only out for what he could get.

Bob got a job working at a car shop.

Rachel went on to buy a brand-new house that was simply gorgeous that would run rings around the first one.

She quit her secular job to take an administrative job. She also continued running her consulting firm.

In honor of her grandmother, Rachel opened up an exclusive restaurant that offered entertainment and dancing.

Rachel's restaurant is a class act. The atmosphere and food are simply amazing.

Rachel has proven that you don't need a man to succeed. Her success came from her willingness not to back down and to give her family a good life.

With or without a man by her side.

Bob's failure came when he turned his back on his wife and kids. How do you repair a family when you don't have a guilt complex.

Rachel is simply an awesome lady. She's all about family.

When she opened the restaurant, her son and daughter were right there with her.

Rachel didn't stop at her kids. She also employed her nieces and nephews.

Is Rachel an over-achiever, or did she just plan well and didn't let anything get in her way, not even her health.

She told me one time she can rest when she die!

Rachel is still on the move. Catch her if you can.

Chapter Twenty

Cynthia

Cynthia is a free spirit. She was not one to be shackled or tied down.

Cynthia is a free spirit. She was not to be held back in no way or form.

Take for instance when she ran away from home at fifteen. She didn't shrink back home out of fear of the big bad world, but rather she embraced the challenge.

Even though Cynthia sought out the streets to get a taste of the world, she never turned to drugs. She may indulge in a drink or two, but she didn't allow drinking to dictate her thoughts or life.

Cynthia owns her own, got her degree. We would have wanted her to go to college and get a degree, but Cynthia had her own plans. She did it her way—she partied a little bit, but she never lost track of her goals or what she wanted out of life.

Cynthia had always been a determined person since childhood until she became an adult. Her strength can be frightening if you haven't developed confidence in yourself.

Cynthia had always been a very smart young lady. We knew at a very young age she would be someone you would reckon with.

Cynthia could've attended college at an early, but she wanted to control her own destiny and that's exactly what she did.

My daughter was dating this young guy that me and my ex-wife liked a lot, but my daughter wasn't feeling his temperament.

They had wedding plans that got cancelled because Kelvin didn't meet up to her expectations.

Kelvin had been instrumental in Princess's life, the little child born with healing powers.

When Cynthia left our home, I had become downtrodden. I was in a state of shock until my princess smiled at me and said, "Papa," then I instantly became part of the living once again.

Cynthia, like I said in the beginning, is a force to be reckoned with.

Cynthia demanded that Kelvin not only take care of his little girl but that he be a regular part of her life. Princess is a beautiful, smart young lady with the world at her fingertips to control.

Chapter Twenty-One

Princess

Let me tell you about my little princess!

I can look back at a time when she was driving her electric car down the street for the first time. It was like she had done it before, as if controlling of the car was nothing new to her.

I know then the power of the world would be nothing for her to conquer.

Princess has been in gifted classes since her first day of school.

She has been excelling ever since. I like to say it was because I used to sit and watch CNN with her and read to her.

She has very smart parents and a grandmother that taught her ABC when she was about three and was teaching her to count.

I guess you can say we all played a part in her excelling in school. But the real credit has to go to Princess and her willingness to do the work upon her mom's insistence on giving nothing but your best.

Oftentimes you are harder on your kids because you don't want them to make the same mistakes you made.

Princess's attitude about life is good, and she wants to be successful which is a plus. If you can't see a future, how can you arrive there in your own time.

Princess has built her own robots in class and masters her classwork at the ease of blinking her eyes.

Princess has won numerous academic achievement awards.

Nothing is holding Princess back but time.

Princess's thought is to go to Harvard. Her mom and dad are okay with anything she chooses to do because so far she has been on point.

My Princess no matter what, remember Papa always loved you dearly.

My job as your grandfather is to make sure all obstacles is out your way, so you can have an easy path to greatness.

The beginning of a great story . . . Stay tuned.

The story of Cynthia continues.

Cynthia accomplished something I never did: she had a house built from the ground up from her meticulous specification.

That dream I have has yet to come true.

She did have me do some painting with her husband Marty. She always kept me in the loop somehow.

Yes, Cynthia had left Kelvin behind and fell in love with Marty with whom she had a baby boy.

All was good and going well—new furniture and appliances, and all the pleasures and conveniences of life anyone can ask for.

Cynthia and Marty had the world at their fingertips: a boy and a girl, and a house built from the ground up. The perfect setup for a new family.

Marty made one vital mistake; he failed to listen to his wife's feelings.

Being the man of his house took precedence over his wife's feelings.

Marty had moved his mom in their home, and now the mother thought she was the lady of the house. Marty was telling her no different.

What a major conscious mistake Marty made.

Cynthia tried her best to understand Marty's feelings toward his mother because if push came to shove, she would have opened her home to her parents also.

Enough was overflowing in time for a change; it could only be one woman of the house.

Cynthia kindly gave Marty an ultimatum. She didn't want her relationship to be put on the auction block, but Marty's hearing aid was evidently faulty. He chose not do anything so in essence he sided with his mother.

Marty, Cynthia's husband and the father of her son, was a fool. He allowed my daughter to walk away because of foolish man's pride. An ego on overload usually causes a crash at some point in life.

It's always a price to pay if you let your pride go unchecked.

Marty loved his son without a doubt, and he had been a true father.

Cynthia told me she was leaving Marty and everything behind.

My reply, "Cynthia, are you sure that's the road you want to go down?"

"Dad my mind is made up. He made the decision. I'm just following through."

Cynthia packed up her kids and clothes and left her humble home and struck out on her own.

She left house and all behind with Marty and his mom.

A house is only a material possession from your success in life. A home is where your heart resides—there's a major difference.

Why would a woman give up everything she built from the ground up?

It was because it's not a home. If love doesn't reside then it's just a house. So she moved on to continue her life journey.

Cynthia was charting a new course in life, and Marty was cut out the picture.

Cynthia got her own apartment and continued raising her kids.

Cynthia wasn't satisfied with mediocre, so she made plans to move to Florida.

I came to help her move. She said, "Dad, you didn't try to talk me out of moving."

I said, "Would it have mattered?" She said, "Probably not, but I'm so used to you giving your opinion."

"My dear, you are grown. You once told me when I interfered in your life. You said to allow you to make mistakes, otherwise, how are you ever going to learn."

Yes, I was sad because my daughter was leaving and my grandkids were leaving too.

In my mind, I knew she would come back. She had never gone that far without family.

How silly I was she left home at fifteen and never came back home.

So what was I thinking?

One day, I got a frantic phone call from my ex-wife. She tells me to take a seat.

She goes on to tell me that Cynthia said her boyfriend tried to take her life.

He began choking her while my granddaughter was in the other room.

My daughter kept her composure because she couldn't put her daughter's life in jeopardy.

Cynthia was able to talk to him and calm him down.

He eventually got tired and went to sleep; that's when she made her escape with Princess and had him arrested.

My daughter still has nightmares and wakes up crying!

I cried because I held my tongue, because I wanted to show my daughter she was an adult and she can make her own decisions without her father's interventions.

I blamed myself because I should've spoken up.

I cried because I wasn't able to exact vengeance as a father is supposed to be his daughter's hero, no matter what her age is.

I have no excuse. I failed her, and for that I can never forgive myself.

Cynthia still didn't come home; she had the boyfriend arrested and went on with her life.

Cynthia has proven without doubt that nothing is going to stop her from obtaining her desires out of life.

Cynthia confided in me she's having nightmares of the incident. She said she wakes up crying for no reason at all.

It was also time for him to get out of prison.

While he was out on parole, he was convicted again, this time for murder.

He strangled an unsuspecting young lady who evidently thought she had the answer to the cure for his aggression.

Most women would've put up an "I hate men" sign and swore them off forever, or they would've climbed up in a shell and let life pass them by.

But Cynthia is fearless and focused on being the best woman she can be, no matter if that entails being a wife or a mother or a career woman.

Cynthia had a mission to complete.

Cynthia meant to have the idea of family, and as time flew by, a new day arose.

Unfortunately, I'm my daughter's friend on Facebook.

That's how I got to meet her new boyfriend who is now is her husband.

My beautiful daughter had met a nice young man who loved her more than himself. His aspirations and positive outlook on life complemented that of my daughter.

Cynthia's life had taken a new shape. She didn't fold when she was faced with insurmountable life issues.

She just saw it as another day in her life. She didn't ponder over the negative but look to her future.

Cynthia made me a very happy dad when she asked me to give her away on her wedding day.

The planning of the wedding was extremely hectic.

Cynthia is very meticulous, and her plans have to be followed to the letter, to the cross of the *t* and dot of the *i*.

If not they would definitely feel her wrath.

Professionalism was required because this was her special day!

My lovely, beautiful daughter stopped the wedding procedure because they hadn't quite decorated the reception hall to her specification.

Cynthia is a meticulous lady; either you do it right the first time or get introduced to her wrath.

The wedding did get underway, and it was simply gorgeous.

I was proud to be hand in hand with my gorgeous daughter. Words cannot describe my feelings.

Everything was simply beautifully arranged, and the wedding was simply beautiful.

The reception was amazing. Everyone was dancing nonstop to the sounds of love provided by the professional DJ.

His music transcended your soul. You had no other choice but to groove to the smooth sounds of the night.

Love had spoken.

Cynthia's life is still going full steam; at this point and time she's planning to open her own restaurant.

Cynthia got her life force from her mom, who we will learn a little about next.

Chapter Twenty-Two

Jill

Jill is a very well-rounded lady. Her achievements in life are remarkable because they weren't without strife.

Jill is my ex-wife, Cynthia's mother.

Even though our marriage didn't work, we remained good friends. You ask what went wrong?

Life in itself is deceitful and treacherous.

Life will set you up beautifully and have everything running smoothly.

Then it will steal your thunder and stab you in the back with past and present unresolved issues.

This causes turbulence and tremors as you try to stabilize your life.

Unresolved issues from the past, they never go away.

They lay dormant like a snake, waiting for the right time to strike.

They cause problems for the here and now. When you add past problems with everyday issues, you get instability, confusion, and disturbance.

Sometimes, beautiful relationships are doomed before they have conceived. You are going to hear this phrase again in a different way because it needs to be repeated so you can get the point.

We have to learn to communicate without borders, without fear of reprisal, and not being afraid whom it may hurt.

Jill is a very, very resourceful lady. Not only is she resourceful, she is also resilient.

We were married going on twenty years.

Jill didn't cave in and give up on life because after we parted ways, she kept afloat.

During our marriage we had our ups and downs, but mostly our union was a partnership filled with love. Still, our failure to keep a focus on what we had caused us to become distraught with life, causing our union to be riddled with insecurity.

Not to mention the matters unrelated to our marriage that caused pain in our hearts.

Jill is very devoted to her family, but it seemed like someone she loved was passing on every other day.

Jill's two beloved aunts died, two brothers died, and she lost her father and two uncles as well.

Jill also lost her nephew Tim way too early, who was only in his thirties, from a bad heart. He could have been saved, but negligence on the doctor's part caused him to pass away way too early.

When do you get a chance to stop grieving?

Jill also lost a nephew way too early. He was in his early forties; she raised him like a son.

No one could stop the outburst of cry from the pain in her heart.

She was distraught at the losses, but she didn't allow it to rule her life nor did she -in to the self-pity fund. However, it did take a toll on her emotions over time.

A lady that is self-sufficient in no way does she take from the helpless fund.

In high school, she was a scholar athlete; she ran track and medal at state.

The coaches had her running against boys because she would leave the young ladies at the starting block.

She was only a freshman at the time she had aspirations to go to the Olympics, but that got cut short because she got caught up with an older guy, got pregnant, and had her firstborn son.

That stopped her Olympic hopes but not her life.

Jill had her baby, but the father took off. He didn't stay around to take responsibility.

I guess going to buy baby supplies and baby milk take years to achieve.

It didn't matter because Jill wasn't about to let her baby suffer or need anything.

Of course, she was disappointed, but as I said above she was resilient.

After school, she got a job at a restaurant and worked up to supervisorial position. She met the man who would become her husband.

Jill had her second born—a beautiful baby girl, who would turn into a lovely lady.

The marriage didn't last because Todd, Jill husband, was unfaithful. He couldn't find his way to his own bed.

Jill loved him, but she couldn't allow him to use her, and he had forsaken his rights as a father.

So she filed for divorce.

Todd begged her not to divorce him, but he continued to prove he couldn't find his own bed; he couldn't be trusted.

Jill continued to raise her kids on her own until we met.

I met her at the restaurant she was supervising. What drew us to each other was our situations. We were both dealing with the same issues.

Over time, we started dating and eventually, we got married.

Jill was a very beautiful bride.

We didn't have a traditional wedding; we got married at the courthouse.

Which bring us up to date why we got divorced.

It wasn't only one thing. It was a lot of intricate things that build up to a landslide under which we couldn't dig out from.

Life is cruel. If anyone tells you any different, then they have a closed mind to reality.

It's good to be positive because being negative will leave you walking in place, but you have to be realistic and remind yourself happiness doesn't come free. You've got to pay a fee by being diligent and going out and seeking it, no matter where its hiding or masquerading.

Jill and I were extremely happy at one point in our life. Then, without looking out the window or asking who is it, we just opened the door to *stress* and its first cousin, *unhappiness.*, Then came *negativity* uninvited, with its date *drama.*

Jill couldn't find her way back into our once-loving marriage.

Jill left me a note giving me my freedom.

I cried like a baby because I thought I lost my family.

My daughter by marriage told me it didn't matter what was happening. She would never forsake her father. Again, I put my hands in my face and cried crocodile tears.

Jill and I parted ways, but the love we had for one another wouldn't allow us to be bitter.

Jill left me with the house and all the furnishings.

She started over from scratch.

Jill was truly a strong lady. Not once did she turn her back on me even though our relationship had been dissolved.

She made sure I was a part of my daughter's wedding.

She told me If I didn't give away my daughter, Cynthia would forgive me, but a part of her heart would remain incomplete.

Jill went on to give my daughter one of the loveliest weddings I have ever attended.

At no point was I excluded or made to look small because I wasn't able to step up as a father should have.

One of the greatest gifts Jill gave me was my daughter and granddaughter and grandson, who both I got a chance to help raise.

Jill during our marriage and after our marriage always excelled on her jobs. She was general manager at three different prestigious restaurants.

At this present time, she is a coordinator at a prestigious hospital earning her way through life in a queenly fashion.

Jill earned more money than most men without a college degree. Proof in itself how important it is to believe in your abilities.

She's proof that a woman can do anything they put their mind to, no matter what obstacle they have to hurdle.

Jill was the best in jumping hurdles at a young age, and she continued to utilize those skills even today.

A lady whose will has no loopholes.

A lady who is loyal to her family.

A lady who is at the beck and call of her aged mom, even though she works at times sixteen hours a day.

Who also has an iron will, most likely where Jill got it from.

Jill never once lost faith in my abilities.

Jill is one of the major reason I'm able to complete one of my dream of being a writer.

A beautiful queen who sees no roadblocks or mountains she cannot jump or climb over.

Jill in no way is passive nor does she understand the meaning of fear or have she ever gave up even though the odds was stacked against her a hundred to one she would always find a way to win.

A lady of physical beauty, as well as in mind and spirit.

The problem wasn't with us; the problem was born before we ever discovered each other.

My pal for life.

Chapter Twenty-Three

Lisa

I never wasted a moment telling Lisa of my feelings.

I wrote about my feelings for her,

In love quotes from my heart.

It hit a soft point in her heart that she said she would remember the quotes forever and never forget whose soul they came from.

She was very gracious.

Not once did she flirt with me or try to take advantage of my weakness because my weakness for her was ever present.

She was unflappable. I couldn't penetrate her amour. She had a state of the art security system that blocked any unwanted love.

Woe for me!

It's not like I was the first guy to try or the first guy to fail.

They all ran away defeated with their tails tug between their legs, wailing like a newborn baby.

She was frank with me she said she was independent and used to being by herself, and that she was stubborn.

My reply was I'm not here to change your life but to enhance it, and I'm also stubborn.

Let the games begin.

A lady who most likely got her strength for survival from death—first from the passing of her mother from cancer then second, from the passing of her beloved father.

All this happened while she was a tender little girl. How did she turn out so wonderful?

Which I knew it crushed her inside every time she thought of them.

Tell me how do you get over the lost love of your mother and father?

She could've easily retired on her infinite crying heart, and no one would've blamed her for doing so.

Instead, she found her strength, rode the waves of her infinite cries, onward to a successful life.

She grew into a phenomenal lady, graduating from college and becoming a boss lady at one of the premier telecommunications company in the world.

She could've gone pro as a figure skater, but she decided to stay and help raise her little brother.

How valiant and selfless of her. No one expected nothing different.

She helped him with many startup and small businesses and inventions, not thinking that she had a life too.

Her goal was to inspire her brother life goals.

I was so impressed.

I had to get to know her better.

So I reached out to her the only way I knew how, and that was through Facebook.

I told her how her mom was instrumental in my childhood, by giving me a smile every time she looked upon me and never failed to say something nice and encouraging to lift my spirits.

Her mother was a beautiful lady, inside and out. She most certainly left her mark on her daughter Lisa.

I had to make Lisa know how I felt. What was I to do?

I bombarded her with love songs after love songs after we got back in touch, after the lost years.

I loved her beauty of heart and because she didn't abuse me mentally nor did she laugh at my cry for her love.

I realized it was one-sided because in the beginning we both texted each other to see how things were going, but as time eroded it became one-sided.

In which I was the only one doing the messaging and calling.

It got to the point I felt she was avoiding me and only humoring me so as not to hurt my feelings by not saying she didn't want to be bothered.

Were my insecurities playing havoc with my affection, for the beauty who strolled back into my life, unaware of my love for her?

Her love was sealed in my heart only to be activated by a failed love and a voice from the past.

At what point does a man give up on love?

Was it the fact that that I never told Lisa I was previously married that caused the descent of our relationship?

A feeling of betrayal or being lied to can be a hard pill to swallow.

Fact is, I never lied to her. I just never mentioned my prior life.

I wanted a fresh start; a perfect virgin love emotionally.

I didn't want it to seem tainted or without valor.

My ex-wife thought she was my only true love in my life.

She was, until our divorce unlocked the chambers of my heart to my first love.

Lisa is a sensational lady who is very family orientated.

I often wondered how she managed to have time to take a breath for herself. She was always at her family and friends' beck and call.

The thing is it's not in her makeup to leave a friend or family in need of assistance, even if she's tired and weary.

A few examples of her merits in life.

She was a caregiver for her father and mother.

I didn't know her father, but her mother was a truly beautiful and sweet lady.

There was never a point in my life when she didn't look on me and didn't offer a word of encouragement along with a beautiful, heartfelt smile saying you are loved.

Lisa not only cared for her mother and father but also for two of her aunts who became ill and died.

She also was there for one of her beloved friend who died of cancer.

A testament to who she was as a person because hadn't she been through enough with the passing of her parents.

Lisa retired at an early age from a job she had worked at for years and was adored.

She could've stayed home and enjoyed life, but she started an online business that was very successful.

Lisa was a very successful Mary Kay consultant.

She had the pink Cadillac styling and profiling.

She wasn't about to rest on her laurels. She decided to help a beloved friend who just opened a preschool. She was one of the most selfless person I know.

Of course there was gossip from the jealous type, those who couldn't match the person she was or from those who wanted her love and felt rejected and became spiteful.

I sign she made the right choice.

I have never seen one person get so much love and accolades on the mention of her name alone on Facebook.

A movie star doesn't get such love.

Lisa is also very humorous and encouraging. Not one time had she fail to lighten my day by just saying hi.

So you can imagine what's going on in her mind when I told her of my feelings of love for her.

Lisa heard me speak of loving her and she read my words but actions speaks louder than words.

How are you stepping to me broker than a fake dollar bill. You can't even afford a complimentary water.

I agreed to meet you and you drive up in your father's car and wearing his suit.

I understand the sentimental value, but what do you own?

I understand you recovering and starting your life over, but I can't support my life on your potential.

I admire your words of love, but you gave me two gifts in four years after we got back in touch.

I know I said you didn't owe me anything, but don't you see a lady likes to be courted even when she says no.

I guess your love's got a budget, and if I were to lose my mind and agrees to date you.

It would be your assumption we would share a dollar cheeseburger and drink, and call it love.

Don't be delusional. I'm not that beauty.

I don't ask for much, but I can't clothe and feed with your love, and I can't drink your potential.

As you know, those aren't her words. Not once has she ever once criticized me—she's been nothing but a rock of support.

My sanity is in check because she said the things that built me up.

Lisa, listened,she never forgot what we talked about. She can recall verbatim what we discussed . . . a charming quality that showed she cared enough to listen.

A good sign Lisa is a good communicator.

Not one time did she question my character or said I couldn't be telling her the truth about the expression of my heart that was spilled out because I knew she would catch them without fear of her using my words as leverage against me.

I allowed Lisa in my comfort zone because she was everything my dreams had ordered and more.

In life, seldom can you find a beautiful lady that's intelligent, and whose character has no inclusion like a flawless diamond.

She taught how to enhance and how to wake up my writing skills.

She never laughed at my broken sentences or lack of correct punctuation.

She always gave me the highest praise and said my skill as a writer is endless. There's nothing stopping me but my mind.

She gave me high praise on my first novel.

With nothing to gain by saying it, she said my first novel without thought in her mind, would be a bestseller.

That remains to be seen.

Did I tell you she was radiant and her beauty has no boundaries?

As time passed, her beauty hasn't faded because her heart has erased any signs of aging.

Her elegance is uncompromising.

Her compassion is without end.

My mind tells me I should walk away and leave her be. But my heart keeps telling me to try and try again.

The battle has begun within me to find love, at what cost?

Will I lose my sanity or will I feed my starving heart?

Walking away from love should be easy when it's not reciprocated.

Walking away from a dream is even harder.

I don't know how to get her to look at me and make me a priority in her life.

Do I love her? Yes.

Am I in love with her? Yes, with every part of me.

What's next for me on the horizon only time will tell it never lies.

I keep calling love but it never ever answers .

Just maybe, Lisa forgot she put her phone on mute .

Maybe this is the time she will answer my call of love ....now it's busy .

I have nothing to lose but time; my heart is already gone.

To be continued!

Chapter Twenty-Four

The Verdict

It's true, famous stars entertain us, make us cry, give our hearts joy and jubilation.

We even often imitate their feat, no matter what it is.

So yes, we want to hear their life story and how they became successful under duress and against the odds.

When they didn't even have the support of their family.

Is it not true they became famous worldwide.

Is it not true their acclaim to fame made them Oscar- or Emmy-worthy. Some even got a Golden Globe or a Grammy.

What do you think about those who won a gold medal or who became champions in their field?

Is it not true they have glamorous houses, diamonds, and gold locked away in safes all over the world in their different homes.

Isn't it true they hide their riches in accounts abroad not just in the States?

Isn't it true they have chauffeurs and the finest luxurious cars money can buy?

Then why was it reported that their millions weren't making them happy?

You shouldn't have a care in the world with all the luxury life has to offer.

Is it not true you hear the famous contemplating suicide?

Wasn't it sad when you heard your famous star committed suicide?

Have you heard of famous names on drugs, like crack, cocaine, and what about opioids?

Did we not hear of their cheating ways and didn't their sexual offenses got them fired and brought about convictions?

I think we put a blanket on most things the rich and famous go through?

Did I not say they were rich and famous and had the world in the palm of their hands?

So how come they couldn't deal with their pain?

Media love to highlight how they overcame some sort of abuse as a child and became famous.

That is truly commendable whenever you can rise above turmoil and affliction of the body and mind and becomes a success story you hear about in movies and read about in books.

I will let you decide knowing all the facts who had the heaviest load and who made the best contribution to society.

I once heard someone say, even though they were abused physically, they knew they were destined for fame.

Sounds good to say and very inspirational to hear.

I believe hard work contributed to their success and dedication to their craft.

I also believe their affliction inspired them to have a better life.

It is not my belief though that while being abused, you know your destiny.

I guess the persons who didn't survive their ordeal would say the same thing if they were alive to say it.

Now let's contrast the lives of the ordinary female with no claim to fame.

Could you relate to their stories?

Were their stories boring because they had no direct link to fame?

All of them had some type of atrocity that happened to them, hadn't they?

They were middle income and had ordinary homes. Some may have been in the suburbs, but in no way could they match that of the rich and famous.

Not one of these ladies sought a life of crime or sought out drugs.

Nor could they be tried in court with any type of sexual offense.

Not one committed suicide or contemplated it.

No, they didn't have intriguing lives nor did they step down in society sewer.

Money or fame cannot buy good morals or keep you from mental or physical pain.

Living a morally clean life can earn you moral Oscar.

Can we simply stop judging people based on their stardom and famous names?

Do they not bleed and get sick and die?

How about judging them based on their contribution to society and how they conquered their demons in life?

They are not idols because they have failures like me and you.

The women I named experienced all types of pain in life, but they didn't bring reproach on their name.

Whatever our situation, we cannot allow the fears in our mind dictate how we live.

Money and fame are supposed to make our life easier. Yes, it may be hectic at times, but isn't ordinary life the same.

It's not the money or fame that's the problem.

It's how it controls us. Do we take control or do we give up our power?

Wasn't it refreshing and faith strengthening to know your pain is not alone even though your name is not mentioned.

This story was about you too.

The everyday ordinary female, who stood up against the odds and didn't put soil on her name, but no one put her name in the lights or on the billboards. You can forget about the Walk of Fame. They didn't take time to learn her name because she wasn't a recognized movie actor. Her name had no claim to fame.

That's funny. Don't they die like me and you? Is that the only time we are on the same level?

Think about it.

Let that marinate!

What travesty. Why isn't our name on the Walk of Fame? Did we not earn our star by our conduct? by not flinching under turmoil?

My Satire / Poetry corner

Chapter Twenty-Five

Disturbed

It's true we all have the right to choose how we live. I'm disturbed by our vetting process in how we decide what road we should take to seek a meaningful life.

Whether man or woman, why would you want to be a notch on someone's bedpost and not a staple in their life?

I'm disturbed because our choices have wide ramifications for all who look in our direction to follow our example.

Even though we have the right to choose, often our choices in life dictate who hears and listen to our voice.

Will it be shallow and weak and have no say in directing our life course?

Or will it be boisterous and loud full of pride because you own the map to your life.

Are you disturbed or are you confident in your eyes directing your course?

There are very few traditional relationships today.

I find it disturbing when a lady says she will never marry a man who has less money than her, but it's okay for a man to marry a woman who depends on his income.

Traditionally, that would be correct. The man would take care of the woman and the woman would care for her man's needs.

It's also true through the passing of time that old fashion values have become extinct in development of character in a large mass of society today.

So why do we stick to old fashion traditional values when they only meet our needs?

Let me tell you how disturbed I am about the death of morality as I see it.

It's a very disturbing fact. We can excuse wrongdoing based on race or one's famous name as a celebrity or sports star, but common people get locked up then after twenty years they get an apology and sets you free because you were found innocent.

Thank you for your time served. Here's a few bucks. Enjoy the life you have left.

If you don't find that disturbing, then you have a malfunction in your heart that can't be healed.

One's race or claim to fame in no way should cancel out his or her stains on society.

Let me tell you about a few conversations I had with who I considered to be respectful ladies.

How can a respectable woman say to me, he can urinate on me anytime he wants with his sexy self.

I ask, do you know the accusation that surrounds him?

Her reply was that's personal then she goes on to try to cancel out his action by bring other people that's been accused and gone untouched.

I ask what if it were your daughter then the room became silent.

In no way or form are you allowed to excuse bad behavior because someone else's notoriety slipped through the crack.

The thing today is to cancel out bad behavior because of race or he or she is my idol and if one goes free they all should get a pass.

I guess the likes of Hitler and Genghis Khan and Napoleon and Idi Amin and let's not forget Osama bin Laden, John Allen Muhammad, Lee Boyd Malvo, and certainly not Helter Skelter or Jim Jones, I guess they should've received free passes because they thought they had a special calling in life. Believe it or not, somewhere they have fans that thinks that's true.

What happened to self-respect? Why would you let a man disrespect and take you out of character for a one-night stand with fame.

On one other occasion, I was having a conversation about the same previous subject.

It's a disturbing fact a middle-aged lady can say to me, "These young girls are nasty. They know what they are doing. They're all about the fame and glory and, let's not forget, they're getting the money."

No man or woman, regardless of their fame or glory, can be excused for their abusive nature. Their money may buy them freedom, may furnish them with a reprieve in life, but it doesn't erase the disturbing revelation twirling of abuse in their mind or who they preyed on.

First and foremost, it's the adult civic duty to turn any child advances away, no matter how of age they may seem to be, or its no way they can relieve you of any responsibility.

How do you excuse an adult but blame a child?

On another occasion I witnessed a disturbing scene.

I witnessed a disturbing group of young people poking fun at each other by using references to male and female genitals and using inappropriate language even adults shy away from using.

It wasn't enough that they were debasing each other; they began to attack and make fun of the adults that were riding along with us while on public transportation.

One young lady who wasn't void of respect said that man hears what you guys are saying.

In reply ‚they said, "We don't care," then they resumed their course of fouling off at the mouth and saying disparaging things to passengers.

No way in my youth would I ever disrespect an adult. How times have changed, that's a common theme I will never accept.

A lady that was in their crossfire had had enough. She was fed up with the disgusting things that was coming out from their voice box.

So she lashed out using vocabulary that upset the kiddies, and that made matters even worse .

The kids reached for their cell phones to call home to Mommy, so she could exact vengeance as if they were quintessential examples of purity!

Everything was about to come to a head as everyone was nearing their stop.

The lady got off her stop early to address the issue with the kids further.

Unfortunately it was the end of the road for me also.

The party escalated because one of the young ladies' mother was coming out of her house.

The lady from the bus was arguing with the child on arrival of the mother; the child took it upon herself to resort to fisticuffs.

The mom stepped in and said, "Why are you disrespecting my child by using foul language toward her? If you have a problem, address me not my child."

In reply she said, "Your child lack the proper home training, so what good would it do addressing you?"

The lady was outnumbered, but no fear was prevalent.

Now along with her precious little girl, she had raised hands.

My signal to step in. I stepped in between the two and said, "Can't you see she is pregnant? This is not happening on my watch tonight."

The mother of the little girl responded by saying, "I'm pregnant too. What about me?" she looked at me as if she was looking for me to take her side.

In reply: then why are we at this point of violence and disgracing ourselves.

The mother backed away and said, "I'll give you this one."

The pregnant lady was full of venom to the point I had to escort her away from the scene.

It's a disturbing fact that some parents no longer have the fortitude to teach their kids the meaning of respect and being responsible for their actions.

No parent knows everything their child is up to, but when we find out, are we scared to be a parent because we want to appeal to our child by staying on their level?

Yes, the morality of the kids today is past shocking. But how were they groomed for society? Did they get a free pass past childhood because their parents weren't brave enough to be a responsible parent.

I am disturbed because kids are acting and treated as adults, and parents are relinquishing their adulthood to stay a kid and avoid responsibility.

As I said earlier, we lose our voice when we make the wrong choices in life.

If we were a drunk, how can we counsel our kids against drinking?

Fact is, the knowledge you have probably is right on point because you are a living proof of the effect it has on a person.

The respect has been lost, so the value of your words is mute.

Do not let your voice be desist or decreased by negative actions of your own doing.

Speak out with love and demand to be heard because now more than ever, our kids need our support. It's not about self-gratification; it's about being responsible for a life that you brought into the world.

Chapter Twenty-Six

Why

Men, why do you abuse the lady you love, then threaten to commit suicide when she rejects your love?

Men, why do we cheat on our queens and cry and deny and say that wasn't me with our pants down around our knees, running down the street. You think inconspicuously, how dumb can one person be?

Men, why do treat our queens like servants and expect a queen's ransom?

Men, why can't we show love and compassion and communicate our love in a proper way, but expect our queens to call us Lord silently in their heart.

Men, why do you feel it's a form of weakness to weep when you feel pain in your heart, yet find strength in tearing down your queen and bringing her to weeping with no end in sight.

Men, we can love our queens without abusing them.

Men, we can love our queens without an outside chick.

Men, we can expect a queen's ransom if we communicate our love to them by showing tender compassion and letting them know without a doubt we would lay our life down for them.

Men, there's no weakness in your tears. Did you not cry when she said I do? Did you not cry when your first baby was born?

Go ahead and cry, and prove you're a man that can show emotions, but at the same time can show strength and protect his queen from harm.

Ladies, why do you allow men to abuse you and deny your beauty to control you, so he could feel like a king and wear a crown he didn't earn?

Chapter Twenty-Seven

My Transportation

My form of transportation does not denote how I will care for you are how I will love you in the long run.

How I love you is not based on my looks or how deep my pocket is.

It's based on my character and my willingness to put your needs before mine.

My happiness is a direct result of making you happy.

If I can't treat you with tender love and compassion, then my love license should be revoked.

We are getting ready to get real.

I had a conversation with two middle-aged ladies. One lady told me under no circumstances could she ever date a guy that has no car.

One other time, I was told by a middle-aged lady who was a bus driver that you she could never date a guy that rides public transportation, who she works for as a driver.

Let's examine what the first lady said why she can't find herself in good faith dating a guy with no car, but she was married to a crack addict with no car or no job.

Now we all know the lifestyle of people on crack. They will do anything to get their high.

I knew of straight guys with families sleeping with other guys for money to get their crack.

This guy in question at one time I highly esteemed him, how people's life changes along with time.

I knew a young lady with a family who did the same thing.

The same lady denied the fact that her husband doesn't cheat on her because he said so. Are we serious? This same guy is gone for weeks at a time, in and out of crack houses, but she trusts his word.

She could be married to a felon, a crackhead, a thief, but she can't in her right mind date a guy who doesn't have a car.

Things that make you go Hmmm!

Her life, her right to use her free choice how she deemed fit.

It doesn't matter if logic lost its eyesight.

Now let's examine why the next lady feels it's beneath her to date a guy on public transportation.

Now I got a friend I used to ride the city bus with to keep her company.

She straight up told me before she met me, she thought she could never date a guy who rode the bus.

After she got to know me a lot better, her train of thought changed because she had seen what type of guy I was and whether I had a car didn't make me or break me.

She told me it was the philosophy of a lot of female bus drivers.

My question to her was what if doctors or other business professionals look down on you because they deem you worthy of their time.

She once told me about this certain female driver who wouldn't even speak to guys because she always thought they all wanted her.

She really was high on her looks and how fine of a body she had.

Now my friend was voted the prettiest bus driver.

By some other drivers who rated drivers by their shapes and looks.

I didn't exactly know this other driver, but I knew what she looked like and all that.

Now when my friend relocated, the other female driver in question voted herself best-looking female driver.

It's okay to think highly of yourself, but at the same time it's okay to be realistic.

In all aspects from head to toe, she was born in denial and she was born with the unfortunate gene.

As I said she couldn't see herself dating a guy who rode the bus.

Now in the area where we lived, doctors, professors, teachers, and administrators rode the bus because they didn't want to pay yearly parking fee. The ones that paid parking fee had to leave their car in a parking lot and catch public transportation to work.

Let me make a long story short. Her boyfriend was a drug dealer.

Again, logic has lost its way.

She said she likes the lifestyle her boyfriend gave her.

None of the other profession wasn't worthy of her time or was it she was insecure in herself.

They could've given her security that her boyfriend couldn't offer because he was always looking over his shoulders.

He wasn't even faithful, so her fairy-tale life was dissolving before her eyes.

Again she has the right to use her free choice and she also has to live with her choices.

We have to stop judging people and start looking at the contents of their heart.

Why not just ask the would-be suitor, whose means of transportation doesn't meet your standards, about his future endeavors, instead of closing the door on him because you summed him up without a word.

There are different reasons why people ride public transportation; don't sell a person below their price even before you find out their value.

It's true, riff raff do ride public transportation, but it's easy to distinguish the two.

My point is if you can't ride with me when I'm down, you certainly can't ride with me when I come up.

Please don't get me wrong. I do understand the queens who take that stand because they got to take advantage if they got the shaft.

I myself would have problem stepping up to a woman with no car or a plan to get around.

I wouldn't want her to think I was a low life and didn't have future plans.

So it would truly bother me because of my pride and reputation would be in jeopardy, not because I didn't count as a man, but because she took me down to a boy because of her false judgment of me.

Because she couldn't see no car she refuses to look at me and find out what I was all about? I could have been her prince charming.

Times have changed. Now you have Uber or Lyft in some areas that's the only people get around because of traffic congestion.

My friend Rachel who I spoke of earlier got taken advantage of to the point that her and her kids' whole livelihood was threatened by her husband. They met in college. You would never catch him on public transportation to conceited for that was beneath him. Yet he had no problem cheating on his wife with several women.

It's okay to love who you love, but make sure they are loving you back faithfully because the one you judge may be your true soulmate who could have fulfilled all your dreams, but you cast him aside because he had a bus pass.

At times we want to sound impressive, and we think we are using sound logic that makes sense only to us.

The two ladies were either in denial of their relationship or they like the so-called bad boys.

Thinking that a man that rides on a bus is a nerd and doesn't have his life together, you see how we can judge someone else yet our feet are soiled and dirty.

Why would you want someone who can only give exciting misery?

Chapter Twenty-Eight

Free Choice

In the brightest light, I couldn't see the darkness that was surrounding you.

The ugliness you glorified yourself with.

Such a gorgeous face, how could this be true of you.

All the things people said about you I denied was right at the onset of meeting you, but I fell in love with a gorgeous face, which lacks character and charm.

A lesson learned not to judge by the outward appearance even though it may be mystifying.

Look away and judge deep within, and see if they have what it takes to nourish your soul with unbiased love and kindness rooted in gold.

Even though you were on your last leg and your beauty had faded, I was willing to be true to you.

Like I promise you when I first laid eyes on you.

The question is would you rather have a man that is broke but will walk ten miles to buy you a Coke?

Or would you rather have a man that's rich but won't feed you when you're ill or get you a glass of water when you have a scratchy throat?

Of course it's your right of choice.

Society puts emphasis on pleasure and material possessions.

For instance, women will allow a man to cheat as long as he brings the bacon home and fulfills her needs.

I would say it's debased thinking; she will say its survival of the fittest.

My reply would be it's a lack of confidence in yourself to do better.

Why would anyone want to share their mate for any reason?

Is it a crime to find a man that's honest and that hears your heartbeats and blows your mind with his dignity?

We have to learn to live and not survive for the next hour or day.

It's true we have free choice to live our life the way we choose.

It's also true we can invite drama and misery free of charge.

It's like enjoying sticking your hand in blazing flame and saying it doesn't hurt. Ouch, it does.

In life, we have unforeseen occurrences that drown our happiness and fame.

So why do we pay the suicide squad with our life free of charge without giving a single dime to a sane life?

A true friend of your heart wouldn't continue to walk on your soul with cleats on purpose.

They would walk away and let the tears fall where they may and allow you to heal.

So you can find someone to absorb your tears and say, "My pain is your pain. We're going to shock the world with unadulterated, pure love."

A smooth-talking man can caress your mind and body so effortlessly and leave you devastated and naked in the cold.

A real man with a stutter will pick you up and clothe you and soothe your soul until you heal. He wouldn't speak a word until you can understand his stuttering.

I-I-I-, uh-uh, lo-love-love you. I only come to love you and rejuvenate your soul.

We have free choices in life, that is true. Please be wise when you choose because your choices can bankrupt and break you down and leave you destitute.

Chapter Twenty-Nine

My Question Is

Why would anyone want to play Russian roulette with the love of your life?

Why would you want to run with the bulls with the one you love?

Why would one want to swim with the piranha with whom your heart belongs?

Why would I want to be a human torch to prove I adore you?

Why would one want to walk on broken glass to prove his or her love for you?

Why would one want to drive into a steel wall to prove his manhood to you?

Why would one want to think they could walk in a lion's den and eat his or her food to prove he has courage and he can protect you?

Why would one think kissing a cobra would be endearing?

Why would one think shaking hands with a bear is recommended to prove you have compassion?

Why would one believe life is reasonable?

The ten things I mentioned are quite illogical, but often we choose to let logic fly away in the wind.

Laws of nature and attraction are not always fair; the question is how do you want to be treated?

The moral of this story is, life is illogical, why give it a crazy pill to enhance its power?

Chapter Thirty

Essential Ladies

A man needs you to love him whether he is up or down.

He needs your encouragement when he is feeling weak.

He needs your guidance when he lost his way.

Essential lady, you are indispensable, you are imperative to his success and happiness.

Essential ladies, never sell yourself to a man, make him work hard and honestly before he can even speak to you.

Essential ladies, study his character, study how he relates to people and how he treated ladies before you.

See if he laughs in support of another man's rudeness or condone disrespect to one's soul mate.

Study how he treats his sister and mom, if he is courteous and respectful.

Essential ladies, do not judge him wholly based on his relationship with his mom.

I know they say the way you treat your mom is how a man will treat his wife.

There is some truth to that, but you also got to consider what type of lady she is and how she conducted herself in front of him.

Did she build him up or tear him down based on her dealings with men in general, or does she judge him and say he's going to be like his no-good father?

Study the closeness of their relationship, but don't judge him on their differences because you don't know what underlying difficulties they had been through.

They also say, Like father like son; that's not a true statement.

Yes, sons do idolize and imitate their dads, whether he's a good father or bad dad.

The key to separation is what kind of man you want to be. A young man my idolize his dad but also recognizes he's not befitting as a father or husband. He acknowledges his dad is not like his uncle or the neighbor down the street.

Who gets greeted with hugs and kisses upon arriving home.

Instead, he's being treated with disdain and disrespect; they regret seeing him opening the door to his car to walk in his home.

Essential lady, a good man recognizes and emulate the good qualities he sees in his father; the bad qualities he allows to evaporate in his mind so they won't have any sticking power.

Essential lady, in her quiet mind, she should never question her sanity on saying "I do."

It's a young man's right to passage to be all he can be by distinguishing himself from his father, by amending the negative with the positive, and by loving his dad and showing respect to him.

By continuing his legacy, by thanking him for the opportunity for teaching him how to be a better man, by not being the man whose blood he inherited.

Essential ladies, communication is a must to find out what's in their mind and heart to find out what intention they have toward you.

People voice their feelings in different ways.

We write when we can't express what we need to say when we can't say it verbally. Is this the coward way out?

Writing allows no interruption and will enable you to jot down your true feelings without a hitch.

Face to face is the recommended approach then you have visual body movements. You can see facial expressions that can tell the whole story in a moment notice .

Essential lady, we love you, you deserve the best life has to offer. Without you we could not be.

Essential lady, we thank you for gracing us with your wisdom and love. If I could give you the world, I wouldn't hesitate to do so.

Essential lady, I bare my heart and soul to you. I cannot see or walk without your guidance.

I cannot see without your light.

I cannot breathe without your lungs.

I cannot heal without your love.

Essential lady, you are the lady I rest my life in.

Chapter Thirty-One

My Queen

Gracious Queens . . .

A man's worth is not based on his looks or height or body weight.

The sum of a man's worth is not what he possesses in his bank account or 401K.

The value of a man is not what he earns in a week or bi-weekly paycheck.

I often heard that as long as the man brings the bacon home and show you some loving, you can overlook his cheating ways.

I'm here to tell you that's some certified triple-A bull crap.

Sit down and have a conference with your dignity and self-esteem, and let them know under no circumstance is my heart or mind and certainly not my cookie for sale or on discount.

Ladies, never sale yourself to a man make him work hard and honest to speak to a queen.

Study his character, study how he relates to people and how he treats ladies.

See if he laughs in support of another man rudeness or condone disrespect to one's mate.

Study how he treats his sister and Mom if he is courteous and respectful.

Do not judge wholly based on his relationship with his mom.

I know they say the way you treat your mom is how a man will handle his wife.

There is some truth to that, but you also got to consider what type of lady she is and how she conducted herself in front of him.

Did she build him up or tear him down based on her dealings with men in general and his natural father.

Study the closeness of their relationship but don't judge him on their differences because you don't know what underline difficulties they been through.

They also say father like son not always true in all cases .

Yes, sons do idolize and imitate their dad whether his a good father or bad dad.

The key to separation is what kind of man you want to be. A young man my idolize his dad but also recognize he's not befitting as a father or husband. He acknowledges his dad is not like his uncle or the neighbor down the street.

Who get greeted with hugs and kisses on arrival home.

Instead of being treated with disdain and regret seeing him opening the door to his car to walk in his home for a kiss.

In her quiet mind, she questions her sanity on saying.; I do.

It's a young man right to passage to be all he can be by distinguishing himself from his father by amending the negative with the positive and by loving his dad and showing respect to him.

By continuing his legacy by thanking him for the opportunity for teaching him how to be a better man by not being the man who blood he inherited.

Ladies Communication is a must to find out what's in their mind and heart to find out what intention they have toward you.

Some people voice their feelings by being verbal, visual, or by the use of a pen or pencil.

We write when we can't express what we need to say verbally.

Writing allows no interruption and will enable you to jot down your true feelings without a hitch.

Then you have visual body movements or facial expressions that can tell the whole story in a moment's notice. You also have inactivity which can say to you what state of mind you are in.

Then you have the preferred way of communication.

Which is verbal; eye-to-eye contact is the preferred way people want to communicate to read how truthful the person is, speaking to see if they have conflict in the emotions in their face which can tell a whole story without uttering one word.

My Queen, you can demand the life you want; the power is in your grasp.

Chapter Thirty-Two

The Power of Reason

The problem with our decision-making is that we allow our physical desire of ecstasy overpower our power of reason.

A lot of times people camouflaged their weakness to promote their strength.

The false impression of strength inhibits our power of reason to make good decisions in life.

There is nothing wrong with the desire of the flesh, but uncontrollable desire can be addictive and lead to decisions based on feeding the desires of your flesh.

Wrongful desires of the flesh and mind tend to take you into uncharted waters, thus challenging to navigate.

Society emphasizes two types of lusts, which are physical and material.

Both cover a range of life topics.

Fighting against popular trends, tend to wreak havoc within, as to which direction to travel.

Then again that depends if you tend to be a follower or be a trendsetter.

Training your mind and body to think logically in a world of confusion could seem impossible.

Once you do the honest research within yourself and society, you will tend to find the chancing of lust of any kind will always take you to the door of unhappiness.

One has to find their balance in life and not try to impress society with traits swaying back and forth, dormant in the wind.

Only in the novels can you see true love you long for in your fantasy.

No man or woman can compete with a book of fantasy. It's simply impossible. How can an imperfect man or woman compete with a perfect fantasy?

One thing to remember: movies on the big screen of unbiased love that gives you unfiltered chills and make you cry because of the tenderness of love that's being displayed. Remember one thing, it's scripted to make you feel what real love should feel like.

An example of life you can have if you put the time in and set the proper course to achieve serenity of life.

Often, movie stars live a different life than we see on the big screen. Certain movies are made to simulate happiness, but we have to decide the difference between make-believe and reality.

It's all right to act out your fantasy as long as in real life, you can make the movies come real in your life.

No doubt for sure we have freedom of choice to decide our fate.

Life choices will guide our steps.

Deflower ignorance, empower your power of reasoning.

Walk in the direction of the light.

Chapter Thirty-Three

Contessa

No one owns or possesses your unwavering love without charge.

His fee is his commitment to love you and respect you, and treat you with royalty, no matter what day or hour because there is no time to waste because of what minute or an hour are we promised.

We will be fortunate to live out our days and who knows how many we have left.

Send her flowers or a gift to say I love you, by not being prompted by Valentine's Day or Christmas or her birthday. Do not allow the need for the cookie to misalign your thinking only to show love and affection when your body text messages you and say, "Let's get it on."

Do not let the greed of society dictate to you how to say I love you to your mate.

Don't let anyone for that matter dictate to you or shame you in not showing love because they loathe affection and respect because they were raised in a pit of self-hate and defecation.

It's true, anxiety and depression play a key role in our lives and decision-making, so why add to our imperfect makeup by adding someone to your life who cannot authenticate his or her love for you?

Who therefore cannot begin to think about loving you for who you are unconditionally, not even for a fraction of a second.

Contessa, find a love who will treat you like the royalty you are, like there are no other beautiful women in the room.

Contessa, remain royal and true to your calling for any man that loves you have found untold riches; he is golden.

Chapter Thirty-Four

Love Without

Love without borders or walls
Love without being contrite and loathing
Love without prejudice of family
Love without failure to apologize and go to bed mad
Love without the cruelty of any type
Love without being a shame to show love without unfair expectations
Love without being territorial
Love without tainted emotions
Love without being misleading about one's true feelings
Love without being demanding and on a power trip
Love without showing disrespect on purpose
Love without playing emotional games that cause unnecessary hurt
and drama
Love without being a commander or dictator
Love without having evil intent
Love without being selfish
Love without baptizing with a spiteful tongue
Love without judging
Love without failure to be pure with your feelings
Love without losing control of one's goal in life
Love without a bitter heart toward the one you say you love

Love without keeping alive the injury from the past.

Love without extinguishing the flames of agape love.

Love by showing appreciation and honor, and by being attentive to her body. Know when she's hurting mentally and physically. Be appreciative of her passions for no reason at all.

My beautiful lady, never doubt your ability to reign supreme.

Chapter Thirty-Five

Love at What Cost

1. At what cost do we seek true love?
2. Do we wager our body or mind or both for love?
3. Is love mental or physical or both?
4. Can you be in love without showing true feelings?

The Answers

1. True love is priceless!
2. We love with our emotions; no doubt love is mental. So yes, we pay a large wage mentally. Physical attraction or infatuation isn't love. It's a biological attraction to be together by mating or just by holding hands, walking in the park.
3. Sex is indeed physical, but it doesn't equate to love, don't get it confused.
    Having sex or making love or physical acts of affection that can consummate into love.
4. The simple answer is yes, you can be in love without showing true feelings.

Whatever reason that a person may not show feelings doesn't mean they aren't capable of love.

It could be traced back to childhood or maybe they have a psychological disconnect of some sort, but you'd know they love by their actions.

It could be that you were taught to show compassion or affection was a sign of weakness.

Totally my opinions, Disagree or Agree, your choice.

Chapter Thirty-Six

Exquisite Ladies

The sun and the moon are indeed exquisite with their unique rays of light.

The stars in the galaxy are amazing to watch, who can turn away from such beauty?

Roses, gardenia, they are exquisite, are they not?

Like the time I first met you, working at the restaurant, I said to myself, "She is indeed exquisite, is she not?"

We started to talk and found out we have similar problems in life, so we saw the need to mend each other's hearts.

A few months had passed and we found ourselves in love.

We eventually got married after we said, "I do, I love you more."

We had a lovely start with a blended family in a beautiful home.

For some apparent reason, we started to experience turbulence, something all marriages go through.

We tried to bypass it, but it kept getting stronger and stronger .

So a decision was made to jump ship and maybe when we land we would find each other again.

It was not to be. Our hearts had landed in separate places, trying to figure out where do we go from here.

Not at one time did we say bitter words about each other or regret ever meeting and saying, "Hi can I buy you lunch?"

A lot of time has passed, over nine years. I used to think I lost everything I invested my life in, but I found that not to be true.

Because I found a friend for a lifetime. I wouldn't be where I am if she didn't continue to show love for me when I was lost.

True love never becomes bitter.

Only fake love can hold that trophy.

Exquisite she still is, as lovely as she was when I first met her.

Chapter Thirty-Seven

I Love

I want a love that will give me a chill at a single touch.

I want a love that smiles and says, "In you my heart is safely at rest."

I want a love that understands, I will obey when her heart calls to me.

I want a love that will help me be a better man!

I want a love that is undeniably precious that I can spoil and cherish her very existence.

I want a love I can trust that she will allow me to take care of her if she was to fall ill for any reason.

I want a love that will trust me with her deepest, darkest secrets.

I want a love that will not allow me to have self-pity when I'm down but to encourage me and motivate me to stand up on my own.

I want a love that can show me love behind closed doors and in front of her peers and especially her family.

I want a love that's in love with me because I treat her phenomenally.

Chapter Thirty-Eight

Phenomenal Woman

Phenomenal woman she is without doubt, she is in the head of her class.

Phenomenal woman she is, no one can deny how silky smooth she moves.

Phenomenal woman she is, when she speaks everyone stands to give an ovation.

Phenomenal woman she is, when she walks she has a certain way, she swirl her hips that leave men in a trance and make women want to imitate her. It's not that she's flirting or over confident. She is just being herself, the reigning queen that she is.

Phenomenal woman she is, with all her crown and glory, she treats no one like they were beneath her even though she has no equal.

Phenomenal woman she is, I will walk to the end of the earth and back, to prove there is no destiny too far, to prove that my love is tried and true.

Phenomenal woman she is, in her mind she questioned her beauty or was she just being modest? I'm here to tell you without doubt, she is beautiful, her beauty captured my soul and heart.

Phenomenal woman she is, when my day is in a dark abyss, just the thought of her lifts me up, making feel like I can fly.

Phenomenal woman she is, I'm so thankful I've been graced by her as she calls me her friend K.

Phenomenal woman she is, it's been over forty years and I just said, "Hi. I'm in love with you, with who you are as a person," but it was to no avail. She said she appreciates me only as a friend, but time has passed us by.

Phenomenal woman she is, I will leave her in peace, so I can quiet the drumming of my heart.

Chapter Thirty-Nine

I'm a Loving Man

I'm a loving man, but I'm alone sitting in my room scrolling.

I'm a loving man, but I can't find that special lady to cook for even though they say it's one of the main things women find in a man that's sexy, but I find myself eating alone.

I'm a loving man who has an unsightly scar under my left eye.

I was blindsided by a drunk driver, my car was demolished.

It was said I should've been dead.

I woke up in the hospital with blood running down my face with the doctor picking glass out my face.

Someone close to me said, "You're going to be scarred for life. Who's going to want you now?"

I'm a loving man who has silky gray hair. I don't look my age, but I find myself dying my hair to attract that special woman's attention, but shouldn't she want to be original?

I'm a loving man some consider me conceited and boujee. They are unaware that's my charisma at play, so they shy away.

I'm a loving man who was told at one time I need to be making six figures to be considered.

I bought a gorgeous lady beautiful roses in a Cinderella slipper and surprised her with decadent chocolates on another occasion. I assume she was ecstatic at the thoughtful gesture.

To the point she inquired about me to both of our friends. I don't know what story they told her, but she stayed her distance from me. Never said thank you for the chocolates or roses, wouldn't that have been the thing to do? It was evident she was manipulated.

Jealousy had showed its ugly head, but the ladies in question weren't quite draft ready yet.

Neither was the lady of my desire because she didn't have a mind of her own.

I'm a loving man, they say I dress to kill, and I look dashing in my clothes, yet I still dance to love songs alone.

I'm a loving man, yet I still find myself alone; no kids to hug, no grandkids to spoil.

All alone sitting in my window sill, l am listening to my favorite songs.

Rinse and repeat!

I wonder if I could push the Restart button or is this my life? To die alone and without being loved?

Chapter Forty

My Pain

One of the worst pains is to lose someone you love in death or by separation of lives.

It pains me to see my father die right before my eyes . . . powerless to even give him an extra second of life.

It pains me to see the discontent in my family.

It pains me to see my grandmother unaware who her kids or grandkids were.

One of the worst pains I had when my son and daughter ran away from home.

It pains me my son wanted to call his dad and say hi .

It pains me every time I think I could've lost my daughter because a fool wanted to choke the life out of her.

It pains me to see my mother to have to live a life on her own.

The worst physical pain I ever had started from my head down to my legs.

The most excruciating pain I ever felt.

I thought my head was going to burst.

It paralyzed me for up to five minutes, I could not move a limb.

I finally broke free, but the pain was persistent.

I was crawling around on the floor saying, Is this the end of me?

I fought for my life because I couldn't let anyone find me like that, and I had yet to leave my legacy behind.

This the first time this story has been told.

Chapter Forty-One

Love/Serenade

Love, forsaking your needs to fulfill the needs and wants of the one whose air you breathe.

Love is not racist or superficial or without tears.

Love protects, communicates, nourishes the soul, physically and mentally.

Love is honest without abuse, attentive and patient.

Love is a beautiful walk in the sunset or just holding hands while strolling on the beach, watching the gorgeous view of the tide coming in.

Love is being crazy and running in the rain and throwing snowballs. Love is anything you want to make as long as you're doing it with the one you promised you would die for.

Love is simple but complex; in order to live at some point in life, you have to have experienced love. If not what's the point of life?

Serenade

Typically a man serenades, but love lends its voice to the ladies also.

My love, I fail in love even more after the first time you said hi.

I knew it was real when my dreams of you came true.

My love, time erodes as we grow older, but my love just took its first breath at the first glance at the beauty within you.

My love, at the first glance of your hazel eyes, you put me in a trance.

The very thought of you calling my name turns my fantasy into a dream come true.

Oh, how I wish I could go back in time and wipe all your tears away and tell you how Gorgeous you are and tell you how much I love you and adore you, but you know that by now.

If I have to, I will love you from afar, to show you my love won't expire.

They say a man ain't supposed to beg, but when it comes to love, you have to give all you've got.

Sounded like I heard a maybe, let's give a trial run.

I'm down on my knees asking you, let me breathe for you?